AQA

Religiou
Studies A
Roman Catholicism

GCSE

Peter Wallace

Series editor

Cynthia Bartlett

Nelson Thornes

Published in 2009 by:
Nelson Thornes Ltd
Delta Place
27 Bath Road
CHELTENHAM
GL53 7TH
United Kingdom

09 10 11 12 13 / 10 9 8 7 6 5 4 3

A catalogue record for this book is available from the British Library

ISBN 978 1 4085 0457 4

Cover photograph/illustration by Alamy / Picture Contact

Illustrations by Paul McCaffrey (c/o Sylvie Poggio Artists Agency)

Page make-up by Pantek Arts Ltd, Maidstone

Printed and bound in Croatia by Zrinski

Photo Acknowledgements
Alamy: ArkReligion.com / 6.6A; Dave Wilkinson / 3.9B; Photospin Inc / 2.11A; Steve Skjold / 4.8A; The London Art Archive / 4.5A; **Ark Relgion:** CCP / 1.13A; Helene Rogers / 2.9B; 3.5B; 3.5C; 5.5C; 5.11B; 6.5B; Keith Cardwell / 3.6A; **Bridgeman Art Library:** William Blake / 1.4A; **British Library:** 1.1B: **Corbis:** CorbisKuwait / Kai Pfaffenbach / Reuters 5.2A; CorbisMetropolitan / Marko Djurcia / Reuters 5.8A; Dan Forer / Beateworks / 3.6B; Rober Mulder / 5.7B; **Fotolia:** 1.1A; 1.9B; 1.10A; 1.10B; 1.12A; 2.3A; 2.6A; 2.7A; 2.8A; 2.12A; 3.7A; 3.9A; 3.10A; 4.1A; 4.2B; 4.3A; 4.3B; 4.6B; 4.7A; 4.9A; 4.10A; 5.1B; 5.4B; 5.5B; 5.8B; 6.4B; 6.5A; 6.6B; 6.8B; **iStockphoto:** 1.3A; 1.5A; 1.5B; 1.6A; 1.6B; 1.7A; 1.8A; 1.9A; 1.11A; 1.11B; 2.2A; 2.4A; 2.7B; 2.9A; 2.10A; 3.1A; 3.1B; 3.2B; 3.3B; 3.3C; 3.4A; 3.4B; 3.5A; 3.7B; 3.8A; 3.8B; 3.8C; 4.2A; 4.2A1; 4.4A; 4.4B; 4.6A; 4.11A; 5.1A; 5.3A; 5.4A; 5.5A; 5.6A; 5.7A; 5.9A; 5.11A; 6.1B; 6.2A; 6.3A; 6.4A; 6.7B; 6.8A; **PA Photos:** 3.10B; **Peter Wallace:** 4.9B; **Salvation Army:** 5.10A.

Text Acknowledgements
Scripture quotations taken from the Holy Bible, New International Version. Copyright © 1978, 1984 by International Bible Society. Used by permission of Hodder & Stoughton, a division of Hodder Headline Ltd. All rights reserved. "NIV" is a registered trademark of International Bible Society. UK trademark number 1448790.

1.5 The English translation of The Apostles' Creed by the International Consultation on English Texts used with permission. 2.1 Excerpts from the English translation of Rite of Baptism © 1969, International Committee on English in the Liturgy, Inc. (ICEL); excerpts from the English translation of The Roman Missal © 1973, ICEL; excerpts from the English translation of Rite of Confirmation (second edition) © 1975, ICEL; excerpt from the English translation of Rite of Marriage © 1969, ICEL; excerpt from the English translation of Rite of Penance © 1974, ICEL; excerpt from the English translation of Ordination of Deacons, Priests, and Bishops © 1975, ICEL; excerpt from the English translation of Pastoral Care of the Sick: Rites of Anointing and Viaticum © 1982, ICEL. All rights reserved. Used with permission. 3.8 Extract from The Spire Magazine, St James's Church, Hampton Hill, TW12 1DQ used with permission. 3.10 Extract from the Student Cross Organisation (registered charity number 1019313) website used with permission. 5.9 Extract from The Salvation Army website: © The Salvation Army, used with permission.

Contents

Nelson Thornes has worked in partnership with AQA to make sure that this book offers you the best possible support for your GCSE course. All the content has been approved by the senior examining team at AQA, so you can be sure that it gives you just what you need when you are preparing for your exams.

How to use this book

This book covers everything you need for your course.

Learning Objectives

At the beginning of each section or topic you'll find a list of Learning Objectives based on the requirements of the specification, so you can make sure you are covering everything you need to know for the exam.

> **Objectives**
> **Objectives**
> **Objectives**
> **Objectives**
> First objective.
> Second objective.

AQA Examiner's Tips

Don't forget to look at the AQA Examiner's Tips throughout the book to help you with your study and prepare for your exam.

> **AQA Examiner's tip**
> Don't forget to look at the AQA Examiner's Tips throughout the book to help you with your study and prepare for your exam.

AQA Examination-style Questions

These offer opportunities to practise doing questions in the style that you can expect in your exam so that you can be fully prepared on the day.

AQA examination questions are reproduced by permission of the Assessment and Qualifications Alliance.

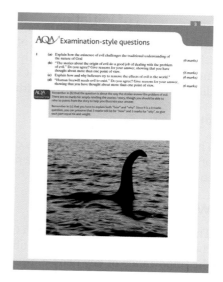

Visit **www.nelsonthornes.com/aqagcse** for more information.

AQA GCSE Roman Catholicism

This book is written specifically for GCSE students studying the AQA Religious Studies Specification A, *Unit 3 Roman Catholicism*. The unit is based on what the Roman Catholic Church teaches and practices, and how these teachings and practices affect the lifestyles of believers.

You do not need to have any prior knowledge of or personal commitment to the Roman Catholic faith to study this course. You simply need to be interested in gaining a knowledge and understanding of the basic principles and practices of the religion. The unit will provide you with the opportunity to develop this knowledge and understanding. While the emphasis is on Roman Catholic belief and practice, the unit will also examine the common ground that all Christians share, and the distinctions between the Roman Catholic, Orthodox and Protestant traditions.

■ Topics in this unit

In the examination you will be asked to answer five questions out of six that are based on the following six topics:

Beliefs and sources of authority

This topic considers the key beliefs and sources of authority that underpin the Roman Catholic way of life and influence Catholics' behaviour and attitudes.

Sacraments of initiation

This topic considers the process of initiation, whereby a person becomes a fully committed member of the Roman Catholic Church, and the different practices of baptism within Christianity.

Places of worship

This topic considers the features of different places of worship and pilgrimage, with particular reference to the Roman Catholic tradition.

Worship

This topic considers how Roman Catholics practise their faith in both private and public worship, and the importance of key people, prayers and aids to worship in the life of a believer.

The Eucharist

This topic considers the centrality of the Eucharist in the Roman Catholic and other Christian traditions, and the impact of the Eucharist on the life of a believer.

Festivals

This topic considers the key events in the liturgical year for Roman Catholics and how these influence their beliefs and lifestyle.

■ Assessment guidance

The questions set in the examination will frequently require you to show a knowledge and understanding of Roman Catholic Christian beliefs and responses. The questions will sometimes require you to give examples of different Christian responses, though these need not necessarily be opposing responses. Each chapter has an assessment guidance section at the end. It will help you to write better answers yourself, if you understand what the examiners are looking for when they mark these questions. To assist you in this, you will be asked to mark an example for yourself – using the mark scheme below. Make sure that you understand the differences between the standard of answer for each level, and what you need to do to achieve full marks.

Examination questions will test two assessment objectives:

AO1	Describe, explain and analyse, using knowledge and understanding.	50%
AO2	Use evidence and reasoned argument to express and evaluate personal responses, informed insights, and differing viewpoints.	50%

The examiner will also take into account the quality of your written communication – how clearly you express yourself and how well you communicate your meaning. The grid opposite also gives you some guidance on the sort of quality examiners expect to see at different levels.

Levels of response mark scheme

Levels	Criteria for AO1	Criteria for AO2	Quality of written communication	Marks
0	Nothing relevant or worthy of credit	An unsupported opinion or no relevant evaluation	The candidate's presentation, spelling, punctuation and grammar seriously obstruct understanding	0 marks
Level 1	Something relevant or worthy of credit	An opinion supported by simple reason	The candidate presents some relevant information in a simple form. The text produced is usually legible. Spelling, punctuation and grammar allow meaning to be derived, although errors are sometimes obstructive	1 mark
Level 2	Elementary knowledge and understanding, e.g. two simple points	An opinion supported by one developed reason or two simple reasons		2 marks
Level 3	Sound knowledge and understanding	An opinion supported by one well developed reason or several simple reasons. **N.B. Candidates who make no religious comment should not achieve more than Level 3**	The candidate presents relevant information in a way which assists with the communication of meaning. The text produced is legible. Spelling, punctuation and grammar are sufficiently accurate not to obscure meaning	3 marks
Level 4	A clear knowledge and understanding with some development	An opinion supported by two developed reasons with reference to religion		4 marks
Level 5	A detailed answer with some analysis, as appropriate	Evidence of reasoned consideration of two different points of view, showing informed insights and knowledge and understanding of religion	The candidate presents relevant information coherently, employing structure and style to render meaning clear. The text produced is legible. Spelling, punctuation and grammar are sufficiently accurate to render meaning clear	5 marks
Level 6	A full and coherent answer showing good analysis, as appropriate	A well-argued response, with evidence of reasoned consideration of two different points of view showing informed insights and ability to apply knowledge and understanding of religion effectively		6 marks

Note: In evaluation answers to questions worth only 3 marks, the first three levels apply. Questions which are marked out of 3 marks do not ask for two views, but reasons for your own opinion.

Successful study of this unit will result in a Short Course GCSE award. Study of one further unit will provide a Full Course GCSE award. Other units in Specification A which may be taken to achieve a Full Course GCSE award are:

- Unit 1 Christianity
- Unit 2 Christianity: Ethics
- Unit 4 Roman Catholicism: Ethics
- Unit 5 St Mark's Gospel
- Unit 6 St Luke's Gospel
- Unit 8 Islam

- Unit 9 Islam: Ethics
- Unit 10 Judaism
- Unit 11 Judaism: Ethics
- Unit 12 Buddhism
- Unit 13 Hinduism
- Unit 14 Sikhism

1.1 The Bible: its contents

What is the Bible?

The word 'bible' comes from the Greek word *biblion* meaning 'book', but the **Bible** is not a single book. The Roman Catholic **Church** recognises 73 books in the Bible, written between approximately 1000 BCE and 100 CE. Because of this long period of writing, the individual books were written for different audiences and for different purposes. The Bible contains stories, prayers, prophecies, history, advice about how to live, and poetry, including at least one love poem.

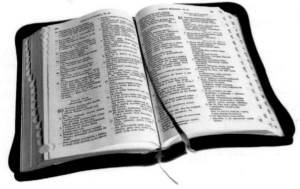

 The Bible

The Old Testament and the New Testament

The **Christian** Bible is divided into two main units: the Old Testament and the New Testament. A testament is an agreement or a promise.

The Old Testament

The Old Testament deals with the way God looked after the Jewish people throughout their history, before the coming of **Jesus**. Christians believe that the promises God made to his people were later fulfilled in Jesus. God guided the Jews throughout their history, protecting them and sending them messengers (prophets) to warn them when they were going wrong.

The Old Testament contains the following:

- The **laws** (Torah): the first five books, dealing with the way God made the Jewish people his own and guided them as to how they should live. These include the Ten Commandments, summarising how God wants people to act.
- The **history books**: showing how God's guidance has always been available if the people were prepared to listen. These can show modern people how to avoid making the same mistakes as their ancestors.

Key terms

Bible: sacred book of Christians containing both the Old and New Testaments.

Church: members of a particular Christian denomination / tradition.

Christian: someone who believes in Jesus Christ and follows the religion based on his teachings.

Jesus: first century Jewish teacher and holy man, believed by Christians to be the Son of God.

Apostles: disciples of Jesus who became the leaders of the Early Church. The word means 'sent out'.

 Papyrus fragment of John's Gospel

- The **wisdom books**: including the prayers (psalms), which show people how to use God-given talents to do what is right in life to be able to stay close to God.

- The **prophets**: inspired figures sent by God to show the people of their times how God is active in the world and to challenge people to stay faithful to God.

The Jewish leaders accepted the books of the Old Testament as inspired by God before the Christians selected their own books in the New Testament.

The New Testament

The New Testament is based on the life and teachings of Jesus and the Apostles. The New Testament can be divided into four sections:

- The **Gospels** (Matthew, Mark, Luke and John) that tell the actions and teachings of Jesus.

- The **Acts of the Apostles** (a continuation of the Gospel of Luke) that tells of some of the events in the early Church up to about 60 CE.

- The **letters** (or **Epistles**), particularly of Paul but also of Peter, James, John and Jude, that show Christians how to live by Jesus' teachings and what it means to be a Christian.

- The **Book of Revelation**, an apocalyptic book dealing with John's visions of the reign of God and the defeat of evil.

These books were not the only early Christian writings. It took about 350 years for these books alone to be accepted as an authentic record of Christian beliefs. There were four important criteria by which particular books were accepted (or rejected) into the New Testament:

- The work had to go back to the Apostles themselves. (Mark was accepted as the scribe of Peter and Luke as based on Paul's witness.)

- It had to have an early date.

- The work had to agree with other presentations of Christian beliefs.

- It had to be accepted by all Christian churches.

These criteria explain why Christians trust what is contained in the New Testament. Other documents, such as *The Gospel of Thomas*, *The Gospel of Barnabas* and *The Gospel of Jude* were rejected very early on because they were written later and did not reflect what Jesus taught.

Activities

5 a Which books are accepted as part of the New Testament?

   b Explain why.

6 'Everything that is contained in both the Old and New Testaments should be accepted equally by Christians.' Do you agree? Give reasons for your answer, showing that you have thought about more than one point of view.

Summary

You should now be able to explain how the Bible is structured and how the books in the Bible are seen by Christians as sources of authority.

Activities

1 What types of books are contained in the Old Testament?

2 'The Old Testament books contain nothing that Christians need.' Do you agree? Give reasons for your answer, showing that you have thought about more than one point of view.

Extension activity

1 Explain ways in which Christians may use the Old Testament to help them understand the Christian faith.

AQA Examiner's tip

You do not have to know the books of the Bible but you should be able to refer to the four Gospels and the New Testament letters (though not by name).

Activities

3 Draw a diagram of the books of the Bible. Identify the contents of the books as law, history, wisdom, prophecy, Gospel, letters and revelations.

4 Is it important to know what type of writing each book of the Bible contains? Explain your answer.

Extension activity

2 'Only the Gospels are important for Christians.' Do you agree? Give reasons for your answer, showing that you have thought about more than one point of view.

The Bible: authority and inspiration

The Bible is the word of God

All Christians accept that through the Bible God speaks to all people. This is why the Bible is called 'the word of God'. God's voice does not come through a loudspeaker from the skies but as gentle stirrings within the human heart or brain. This is seen as the **Holy Spirit** inspiring the believers, who respond by accepting the message that is given and sharing it with other people. Because the message comes from God by the guidance of the Holy Spirit, for believers the Bible has a great **authority**. Christians should be guided by the teachings contained in the Bible.

The Hebrew word for 'spirit' is *ru'ah*, which is also translated as 'breath'. According to the Book of Genesis, God breathed into humanity and gave them life; his own life-force was shared with human beings. From then on God has sent his Spirit to guide people. This is called **inspiration**.

A *God breathing into Adam at the moment of creation*

Many people see God working through the events of every day and throughout history. The books of the Bible that show how God has worked in this way help other people to respond to God's actions and words, to learn from God. This is why the history books and the wisdom books in the Old Testament are seen as important today: God speaks through the words and people listen and act on them.

Objectives

Examine what it means to say that the Bible is the word of God.

Understand the relevance of the Bible for Christians.

Evaluate to what extent the Bible should be a Christian's only guide.

Key terms

Holy Spirit: the third person of the Holy Trinity who descended like a dove on Jesus at his baptism. Christians believe that the Holy Spirit is present and inspires them.

Authority: the power to give orders or to influence people.

Inspiration: the guidance from God to write what is in the Bible.

Discussion activity 👥👥👥

Discuss with a partner or in a small group what it means to modern people to say that the Bible is the word of God.

Research activity 🔍

St Paul says: 'All Scripture is God-breathed and is useful for teaching' (2 Timothy 3:16). Find five passages of scripture that have been used by Christians either for teaching or as the foundation of their faith. Show how the chosen passages have been used.

The prophets and the word of God

The prophets were able to see God at work in a special way. They saw their task was to raise the awareness of everybody to the call from God for the people to stay faithful to him. The underlying message that they gave is still relevant to believers today.

The Gospels and the word of God

Christians believe that Jesus is the word of God made flesh. In Jesus, God speaks directly to all people. The Gospels present the teachings and actions of Jesus, the Word-made-Flesh, so that the Gospels are in a very special way the word of God.

The Epistles and the word of God

The Epistles (or letters) are the writings of the Apostles, the early witnesses to Jesus. They were written to help Christians apply the principles of Jesus' teachings and message to their everyday lives. The Apostles were filled with the Holy Spirit, and therefore inspired to preach and teach God's word. The principles that they laid down for the early Christians still apply today.

B *The Holy Spirit guiding an apostle as he writes*

The teachings in the Bible have been found helpful down the ages. Christians have used the Bible as a guide and a resource book for both their beliefs and their actions. The Roman Catholic Church still uses the Bible as a basis for its teachings as God still speaks through the Bible and still guides the Church through the Holy Spirit.

1.3   The Bible: interpretations

Different interpretations of the Bible

All Christians accept that the Bible is the 'word of God'. However, what Christians mean by this phrase differs greatly. Some take it more or less literally, believing that God himself dictated the words to a human writer, while others believe that the human writers were inspired by the Holy Spirit, and that what they wrote reflects their own personality, time and understanding. Between these two contrasting **interpretations** or approaches, known as **fundamentalism** and the **liberal view**, lie a range of different views about how the Bible is to be understood as the word of God.

Fundamentalism

Fundamentalist Christians believe that the Holy Spirit virtually dictated the Bible and that no one should question anything that the Bible teaches. They believe that God is the God of truth and that he would not mislead people in any way. However, they would be willing to accept that, for instance, the ages of Adam's descendants in Genesis 5 might be approximate rather than exact numbers, or that a day in Genesis 1 does not mean exactly a 24-hour period. Fundamentalists would say that where there are apparent contradictions, people do not yet have enough understanding, either of the text or of truth.

A   *How would a fundamentalist explain the story of Noah's ark?*

An extreme form of fundamentalism is **literalism**, which takes the view that every word recorded in the Bible is true as it stands. For example, literalists believe that:

- there were two different miraculous feedings: of 5000 people (Mark 6:44) and of 4000 people (Mark 8:9)
- Jesus knew all the details in advance of his suffering, death and Resurrection (e.g. Mark 8:31, 10:33–34)

Objectives

Examine different understandings of the Bible as the word of God.

Appreciate how different interpretations can affect how the message is received.

Evaluate the validity of each of these interpretations.

Key terms

Interpretation: an explanation of the meaning (of the Bible).

Fundamentalism: belief in the Bible as a factual historical record; miracles are accepted as events that happened exactly as described.

Liberal view: the view that the Bible's authors were guided by God, but, being human, they could have made mistakes, meaning that the Bible is not entirely accurate, and need not be taken literally. This approach focuses on the spiritual truth within parables, imaginative stories and accounts of the miracles.

Literalism: a belief that every word of the Bible is literally true, even when this defines common sense and logic (e.g. Mark 16:18).

Activity

1   Draw a simple line diagram that shows different interpretations of the Bible as the word of God.

- what Jesus says about the ending of the world (e.g. Mark 13:24–27) will actually take place, exactly as recorded
- God actually made the world in six lots of 24 hours (one Anglican bishop once worked out from the Bible that man was created at 9 a.m. on 23 October 4004 BCE)
- Noah actually took two of every animal into the ark to save them from dying in the flood.

The fundamentalist approach rejects any form of compromise with science. If an idea is not contained in the Bible or if it contradicts the Bible, then it cannot be the truth. God has communicated to people everything that they need to know about himself and life, and if they cannot accept it, it is not God's fault but their own.

The liberal view

This approach accepts that the underlying message of the Bible is true and is from God. However, it focuses on the human agents who wrote down God's message and Jesus' teachings. They did this to help people in their own time to believe and respond to the messages of God and Jesus. It is the meaning of the Bible that is of central importance rather than the way in which it is written. The words might be changed depending on the situation, but the underlying message is from God, and is his word.

The liberal view accepts, for example, that there could well have been one miraculous feeding which has been presented in different ways among different Christian Churches. It could be that the Gospel writers, rather than choosing one account of the event over the other, presented two versions of the one event – the details being remembered differently by different witnesses. This approach also accepts that some of the things presented as directly spoken by Jesus (e.g. the predictions of the Passion and Resurrection) might originally have been more general comments to his disciples. It could be that the writers made them more explicit as they remembered and interpreted the events later, or heard accounts from witnesses.

Research activity

1   Read the story of the miraculous feeding in Mark 6:30–44, then write down:

a   how a fundamentalist approach would interpret the story

b   how a liberal approach would interpret the story.

Activities

4   Give **two** arguments in favour of a liberal approach to interpreting the Bible and two arguments against this approach.

5   'A liberal approach to interpreting the Bible is the only sensible approach.' Do you agree? Give reasons for your answer, showing that you have thought about more than one point of view.

Summary

You should now be able to explain how both fundamentalists and liberals interpret the Bible. You should also be able to assess the value of these different approaches.

AQA   Examiner's tip

You need to be aware of two contrasting interpretations of the Bible: fundamentalism (including literalism) and liberal views. You also need to understand that many believers take a course in between these two opposites.

Activities

2   Give two arguments in favour of a fundamentalist approach to interpreting the Bible and two arguments against this approach.

3   'There can be no contradictions in the Bible.' Do you agree? Give reasons for your answer, showing that you have thought about more than one point of view.

∞ links

You can find out what is meant by the Passion on page 130.

Discussion activity

Discuss with a partner or in a small group which is the best approach to interpreting the Bible, justifying your position.

The Bible: how different interpretations influence believers

The problem

Because Christians have different ways of interpreting the Bible, they also have different opinions about how far they should follow the teachings of the Bible in everyday life. They also have different attitudes to modern scientific ideas.

The fundamentalist approach

Many fundamentalists try to live by the Bible's teachings in their everyday lives. They feel that God has shown them what he wants and therefore it is their duty to live by these teachings.

Fundamentalists sometimes have a problem with regard to biblical teachings about how to live life, especially when the New Testament teaching contradicts the Old Testament. For example, Moses' teachings about divorce (Deuteronomy 24:1–4) contradict those of Jesus (Matthew 5:31–32).

Also some teachings seem to be against the values held by most Christians in the 21st century. If fundamentalists are to be consistent, they must try to apply these teachings. An extreme case can be seen in Paul's teachings in the Bible about the role of women.

Beliefs and teachings

Paul's teachings about the role of women

Now I want you to realize that the head of every man is Christ, and the head of the woman is man, and the head of Christ is God. Every man who prays or prophesies with his head covered dishonours his head. And every woman who prays or prophesies with her head uncovered dishonours her head – it is just as though her head were shaved. If a woman does not cover her head, she should have her hair cut off; and if it is a disgrace for a woman to have her hair cut or shaved off, she should cover her head.

1 Corinthians 11:3–6

Fundamentalism and science

Most fundamentalists reject any scientific teaching that contradicts the biblical story of creation, such as evolution. Most fundamentalists reject the Big Bang theory of the creation of the universe, though some try to adapt the scientific approach so that it can fit in with the biblical story (e.g. accepting that the creation of light on the first day was the Big Bang and that 'a day' means a long period of time).

Activities

1. Up to 1963, women had to have their head covered when they went into Roman Catholic churches. Should this still be the case? Explain your opinion.

2. Explain what a fundamentalist approach to understanding scientific theories would be.

3. Explain why a fundamentalist might find it hard to decide which moral teaching to follow from the Bible.

4. 'A fundamentalist approach to living by the Bible is the simplest and the best.' What do you think? Explain your opinion.

A *God the Creator*

Extension activity

Choose **either** the food laws **or** the teachings about women and examine why many Christians feel that these are no longer relevant.

Activities

5   Outline two strengths and two weaknesses of the liberal approach to living by the Bible's teachings.

6   'All the Bible's teachings need to be adjusted to fit into the modern situation.' Do you agree? Give reasons for your answer, showing that you have thought about more than one point of view.

The liberal approach

The liberal approach starts by trying to place the specific texts being studied into the time and social setting of the original writing. Some people claim that this enables them to see which sections to value as eternal truths and which to see as belonging to a specific context that is no longer relevant. Many Christians take this line with the food laws of the Old Testament (e.g. Leviticus 11:1–8) or the laws about personal injuries (Exodus 21:18–36). Equally, many have no problem with Paul's teachings about women (see the Beliefs and teachings box), claiming that they were written at a time when women did not have the status that is accepted now.

The liberal approach, however, does bring with it certain problems. If people start selecting which passages from the Bible they are prepared to accept and which they will not live by, does this mean that they are putting themselves up as judges of the word of God? A simple example of this would be their attitude to divorce. Should they accept the strict line about divorce that Jesus took or should they say that this is no longer relevant and go back to the more lenient Old Testament laws? On what grounds can any decision be made if humans are to decide which of the teachings of the Bible should be followed and which should be rejected?

AQA   **Examiner's tip**

It is easiest to deal with the fundamentalist and the liberal positions by looking at the extreme positions. Just remember that most believers do not adopt the most extreme positions on these topics.

Discussion activity

Discuss with a partner or in a small group whether the way people interpret the Bible should affect the way they lead their lives, explaining your opinions.

Summary

You should now be able to explain how both the fundamentalist and the liberal interpretations of the Bible would affect the way believers live their lives. You should also be able to evaluate the different positions on this issue.

Research activity

Look up the passage from Deuteronomy and the passage from Matthew and examine how each one might lead a believer to take different attitudes to divorce.

The Apostles' Creed: teachings about God

What is a creed?

A creed is a statement of beliefs. The word 'creed' comes from the Latin word *credo*, which means 'I believe'. The first formal creed was the Nicene Creed, drawn up in 325 CE at the Council of Nicaea. This Creed was developed as a list of what all Christians had to accept to be able to call themselves Christians. Creeds are a sign of being united with all other Christians and sharing beliefs in common. It is almost like the rules of a club everyone is expected to accept. There is no compulsion to belong to the club, but if you decide to join, this is what you choose to accept. The Nicene Creed is said at Mass on Sundays and major feast days.

The Apostles' Creed

The **Apostles' Creed** was not drawn up by the Apostles, but it is seen as an essential summary of what the Apostles taught.

Beliefs and teachings

The Apostles' Creed

I believe in God, the Father almighty, creator of heaven and earth.

I believe in Jesus Christ, his only Son, our Lord,

who was conceived by the Holy Spirit,

and born of the Virgin Mary.

He suffered under Pontius Pilate,

was crucified, died and was buried.

He descended to the dead.

On the third day he rose again.

He ascended into heaven

and is seated at the right hand of the Father.

He will come again to judge the living and the dead.

I believe in the Holy Spirit,

the holy catholic Church,

the communion of saints,

the forgiveness of sins

the resurrection of the body

and the life everlasting.

Roman Missal

Objectives

Examine the teachings of the Apostles' Creed.

Understand why Christians need the Apostles' Creed.

Know what the Creed teaches about God.

∞ links

Refer to page 109 for an explanation of what the Mass is.

Key terms

Apostles' Creed: a statement setting out the main beliefs of the Christian faith.

Trinity: the belief that there are three Persons in the One God. The Father, Son and Holy Spirit are separate, but are also one being.

AQA Examiner's tip

Make sure that you know and are able to comment on the points of the Apostles' Creed.

Activities

1 Explain what a creed is.

2 Explain why creeds are important to Christians.

3 'A person can be a true Christian without accepting everything that is contained in the Apostles' Creed.' Do you agree? Give reasons for your answer, showing that you have thought about more than one point of view.

Case study

What the Apostles' Creed means to one believer

Philip is a 40-year-old Roman Catholic.

'I think the Apostles' Creed is a good guide for my beliefs. I know the original Nicene Creed which we say at Mass was made to get rid of people who did not accept what the rest of the Church believed. This is important because I want to know that what I believe is shared by the other people in my Church. I don't want people questioning my beliefs if they are at the same service with me. I am prepared to stand up and argue about religion with anybody who wants to find out my opinion, but when I go to Church, I go to pray, not to argue. Also I think the Apostles' Creed is easier to understand than the Nicene Creed because it does not try to explain the Trinity; it just accepts the idea and moves on. When I question or I am in doubt about what Christianity teaches, I know the Apostles' Creed can put me right. The simple list of beliefs gives me a good checklist that I can tick off, and if I have a question I can isolate the point and then go and look for an answer.'

Research activity

Find out when Roman Catholics use a creed or statements based on a creed.

■ Teachings about God

The Apostles' Creed affirms the Oneness of God and the **Trinity** of Persons. Christians believe that there is only one, all-powerful God. There cannot be more than one infinite being. However, God has shown himself to Christians as three distinct Persons:

1 **God the Father**, the Creator of heaven and earth, the one who gives life to all things.
2 **God the Son**, who came down to earth as man.
3 **God the Holy Spirit**, who is the power of God at work in the world in the hearts of all people who believe.

The idea of the Trinity of Persons but the Oneness of God is a very difficult idea. However, the main point is that God is active and has a relationship within himself; he is not a distant, unmoving force but an active power of love that works in all creation.

Discussion activity

With a partner or in a small group, say how easy you find the Apostles' Creed to understand, justifying your comments.

Activities

4 God as Trinity is often symbolised as a shamrock or as an equilateral triangle. Draw either of these symbols and explain what it is trying to show about God.

5 'The most important thing about God is that he is the Creator.' Do you agree? Give reasons for your answer, showing that you have thought about more than one point of view.

A *A sign often used to represent the Trinity*

B *A shamrock, another symbol used to represent the Trinity*

Summary

You should now be able to explain why the Apostles' Creed is an important statement of faith and what is meant by the Trinity.

1.6 The Apostles' Creed: teachings about God the Son

The Incarnation

Christians believe that humans had rejected God by their sins and only a human being could repair the damage done. However, people are incapable of being totally obedient to God, and so God the Son became fully human in Jesus. He lived a fully human life. However, though he was tempted as all human beings are, he did not sin, and he did everything that God wanted. Humans are so important to God that God the Son took on human nature to help humans get free from the effects of their sinfulness.

Jesus' life on earth started when the Virgin Mary accepted the request from God to be the mother of his Son. God the Son has existed eternally with the Father and the Holy Spirit, but his conception and birth as man happened in earthly time.

If Jesus had had both a human father and a human mother, he would have been nothing but human, so could not live without sin. If he had just appeared on earth, then he would have been an alien, with nothing in common with human beings. Jesus had to go through the fullness of the human condition, from conception to death, for his life to be of any meaning to us. This stresses that there is no point in the human experience that is not known to God.

His birth of the Virgin Mary by the power of the Holy Spirit shows how Jesus is both fully God and fully man. The fact of God becoming man is called the **Incarnation**, which was announced to Mary by the angel Gabriel in the Annunciation.

> **Discussion activity** 👤👤👤
>
> With a partner or in a small group discuss whether the Catholic Church is right to stress the fact that Mary gave birth to Jesus without losing her virginity.

The Crucifixion, Resurrection and Ascension of Jesus

The Crucifixion

Jesus of Nazareth was a historical figure who was **crucified** by Pontius Pilate to keep the Jewish leaders happy. Christians believe that Jesus accepted this horrific death in obedience to God's will.

The fact that he died and was buried demonstrates that Jesus suffered death as every person suffers death. The phrase 'he descended to the dead' shows that Jesus was separated from God in actual death. This separation was brought about because people sinned and rejected God.

The Resurrection

Since Jesus did all that God asked of him to the point of death, sin and the power of death could not hold him. His **Resurrection** shows that the destructive power of sin and death is over. By destroying the power of sin and death, Jesus made it possible for all people to get to heaven.

Objectives

Examine what Christians believe about God the Son.

Understand what these teachings show about the importance of human beings to God.

Evaluate the need for belief in God-made-man.

Activities

1 Explain what 'the Incarnation' means.

2 Explain why, according to Christian beliefs, God became man in Jesus.

3 'It is easy to believe that Jesus was born of the Virgin Mary.' Do you agree? Give reasons for your answer, showing that you have thought about more than one point of view.

Key terms

Incarnation: God taking the human form of Jesus.

Crucifixion: a form of punishment given by the Romans. The victim is nailed to a cross beam, or tree. Jesus was crucified.

The Resurrection: when Jesus rose from the dead after dying on the Cross. One of the key beliefs of Christianity.

Ascension: the event after the Resurrection, when Jesus returned to God, the Father, in Heaven (recorded in Luke 24 and Acts 1).

The Ascension

After the Resurrection, Jesus was fully raised to endless life in heaven. Being 'seated at the right hand' of God means that Jesus Christ, God the Son-made-man, shares in the fullness of God's power, having been taken up into heaven at the **Ascension**.

Jesus lives and reigns as God now and, at the end of time, he will share in the power of God to judge all people. These beliefs are based on material found in the Gospels, for example Luke 24:44–51:

Beliefs and teachings

He said to them, 'This is what I told you while I was still with you: Everything must be fulfilled that is written about me in the Law of Moses, the Prophets and the Psalms.'

Then he opened their minds so they could understand the Scriptures. He told them, 'This is what is written: The Christ will suffer and rise from the dead on the third day, and repentance and forgiveness of sins will be preached in his name to all nations, beginning at Jerusalem. You are witnesses of these things. I am going to send you what my Father has promised; but stay in the city until you have been clothed with power from on high.'

When he had led them out to the vicinity of Bethany, he lifted up his hands and blessed them. While he was blessing them, he left them and was taken up into heaven.

Luke 24:44–51

AQA *Examiner's tip*

Start by learning what the Creed says about Jesus and then look at the importance of each phrase rather than getting yourself confused by thinking of it all in one go.

Research activity

Find out **four** historical details about the death and burial of Jesus.

Activities

4   Why can't Christians give historical details about Jesus' Resurrection?

5   Explain what the phrase 'he descended to the dead' means about Jesus' death.

Extension activity

What historical details connected with the Resurrection can Christians provide?

Activities

6   Explain what Jesus' death and Resurrection show about the importance of human beings to God according to Christian beliefs.

7   'The most important belief about Jesus is that he really died.' Do you agree? Give reasons for your answer, showing that you have thought about more than one point of view.

A *The Annunciation – stained glass window*

B *The Crucifixion – stained glass window*

Summary

You should now be able to explain how God the Son took on the human condition in the person of Jesus, how he suffered and died and rose again. You should also be able to explain what this shows about the importance of the human race.

1.7 The Apostles' Creed: other Christian teaching

Other Christian teachings and their impact on Christians

The Apostles' Creed ends with a series of statements of beliefs that are central to the way Christians live. These are all based on the teachings of Jesus and have to be recognised as important to believers.

I believe in the Holy Spirit,

- **Belief**: The Holy Spirit is the power of God at work in the world in the hearts of all people who believe. He is the one who inspires Christians in their journey and response to God. He is the one who came down on the Apostles at **Pentecost**, 50 days after the Resurrection, giving them the strength to carry on living Christian lives and responding to God's call.
- **Impact**: Christians have to allow the gifts of the Holy Spirit to work in their lives.

links

See pages 54–55 to find out more about the gifts of the Holy Spirit as received by Christians today.

Objectives

Consider what the Apostles' Creed teaches about other issues.

Understand the impact of these beliefs on the way Christians lead their lives.

Key terms

Pentecost: the day, shortly after the Ascension, when the Apostles felt the presence of the Holy Spirit (recorded in Acts 2:1–4).

Discussion activity

1   Discuss with a partner or in a small group whether it is helpful to depict the Holy Spirit as a dove.

AQA Examiner's tip

You have to know what the Creed says. The easiest way to remember the statements is to think about how each one affects a Christian's life.

A *The Holy Spirit pictured as a dove*

the holy Catholic Church,

- **Belief**: All Christians are baptised into the Body of Christ, the Church on earth (see page 22). They are the living members of his Body and it is in and through the believers that Christ works in the world today. The Church is Catholic, i.e. it is universal, covering the whole world, and is united in Christ.

- **Impact**: Christians must act as part of a united body, not as isolated individuals. Christianity is a shared belief, not a personal interpretation of what an individual wants to believe.

the communion of saints,

- **Belief**: Including the **Communion of Saints** stresses the idea that all Christians are holy (saints) through their baptism. They belong to each other and together they form a fellowship of believers that includes all those who believe in Christ, both the living and the dead. The whole Church is united and will one day find its completion in heaven with Christ.

- **Impact**: Christians accept that they are on a journey through life to heaven. Other believers, both living and dead, can help the individual reach the fullness of life, just as the individual believer has to help others in their faith.

the forgiveness of sins,

- **Belief**: **Sin** is the rejection of God. Everyone finds it easier to do what they want rather than what God wants, but usually what they want leads to failure, frustration and loneliness. God-in-Christ, by destroying the power of sin and death, has made it possible for all people to join God in heaven. This is what is meant by **salvation**. Accepting Christ as Saviour and avoiding sin will enable believers to accept salvation and the invitation to eternal happiness. Christ died so that sin may be forgiven.

- **Impact**: Christians have to accept that sin cannot separate them from the love of God, so they should seek forgiveness and be willing to forgive other people who have offended them.

the resurrection of the body and the life everlasting.

- **Belief**: When each person dies they will face **judgement** based on the way they have lived their life. For those who accept God, judgement will be followed by the fullness of life given to each person in the world to come. This is the meaning of the phrase 'the resurrection of the body'; the old bodies are gone but people live in a new way with God.

- **Impact**: The body is holy and should be respected in this life. Equally, death should not be feared but should be seen as the means of entry to eternal life.

Summary

You should now be able to explain how the Holy Spirit, the Catholic Church and the other later teachings in the Apostles' Creed guide Christian beliefs and actions.

Key terms

Communion of Saints: all Christian believers, both living and dead.

Sin: a thought, word or action against the love of God.

Salvation: being saved from, or being freed from, something, such as suffering or the punishment of sin.

Judgement: the return of Christ at the end of the world to judge the living and the dead.

⬭links

You can read about the ceremony and meaning of baptism in Chapter 2.

Discussion activity

2   With a partner or in a small group discuss whether you think it is important to belong to a Church, explaining your position.

Activities

1   Which of these later teachings in the Apostles' Creed do you think is the most important for Christians? Explain your answer.

2   'It does not matter what Christians say they believe. The only things that matter are the things that Christians do.' Do you agree? Give reasons for your answer, showing that you have thought about more than one point of view.

What is the Church?

The **Church** is the group of believers that accepts Jesus as the Christ, the **Son of God**, God-made-man. **The Church as the Body of Christ** performs the work of Christ on earth now and helps other people to respond to the teachings of Christ. Believers are people who not only follow Jesus' teachings but direct their lives in the light of all that Jesus came to show.

Although all Christians accept Jesus as their Saviour, there are divisions within the Christian community. These divisions have a historical basis but they are made deeper by different practices that are not easy to reconcile.

A *Believers together*

The earliest split, over the role of the local bishop and the role of the Pope, came in the 11th century CE between Christians in Eastern Europe and those in Western Europe:

- The Christians in Greece, Russia and other eastern countries form the **Orthodox Churches**. Orthodox means 'right teaching' and they believe that their interpretation of certain rules is more in keeping with the teaching of the Apostles.
- The **Catholic Church** is in the west of Europe. Catholic means 'worldwide', and the Catholic Church tried to keep all believers in one Body.

The teachings of the Orthodox and Catholic Christians on many issues are very close. However, Orthodox Christians tend to be much more elaborate in their services and stress the holiness and remoteness of God a little more than the Catholics do.

The Church after the Reformation

In the 16th century some Christians protested about the way the Pope in Rome was leading the Church. These **Protestants** broke

Objectives

Examine the different Christian denominations and how they arose.

Understand the different positions taken by denominations on matters of faith and practice.

Key terms

Church: the Holy People of God, also called the Body of Christ, among whom Christ is present and active.

Son of God: in mainstream Christianity the title of Son of God is used to describe Jesus as a divine being and a member of the Trinity.

The Church as the Body of Christ: the belief that the Church is God's people and that it is present wherever people are living a Christian life.

Orthodox: the most popular Christian tradition in some parts of Eastern Europe. Services are heavily traditional and ritualistic.

Protestant: the Churches that 'protested' against and broke away from the Roman Catholic Church during the Reformation. Services are generally based more closely on the Bible than those of the Roman Catholic and Orthodox Churches.

Roman Catholic: the tradition within the Christian Church which is led by the Pope.

∞ links

You can find out about the role of the Pope on pages 26–27.

away from Rome and formed separate Churches. This is known as the Reformation. The majority of Christians in the world still accept the role of the Pope as leader of the Church and are called **Roman Catholics** because of this.

The Protestants formed different groups depending on what they regarded as the most important source of authority:

- The **Church of England** (Anglicans) accept the role of bishops as leaders of the church. However, they also accept the Queen (or King) of Britain, not the Pope, as the overall leader.
- **Methodists** were founded in the 18th century by John Wesley. They believe that the local Christian community should run itself. While they have ordained ministers, regular Holy Communion services and baptism, many Methodists do not hold Holy Communion services each week. Instead they usually attend Sunday services that are based on the Bible and sermons.
- **Baptists** emphasise the importance of one of the sacraments, baptism. They believe that all Christians are equal through their baptism. They only accept baptism for believers, not for babies. They also have Holy Communion services, often once a month. Their main source of authority is the Bible.
- The **United Reformed Church** have ordained ministers but firmly believe in the idea of local churches running themselves, without any central authority. Most decisions are made locally, which makes the Church meetings very important. They believe that all Christians are personally guided by the Holy Spirit. They baptise and celebrate Holy Communion.

The Bible is also central for many of the Protestant denominations that do not believe in the need for an ordained ministry. For example:

- The **Salvation Army** was founded by William Booth in the 19th century. Their belief is expressed in the preaching of the gospel, in music and in community service. They meet on Sundays to reflect on the scriptures and to pray together.
- The **Society of Friends (Quakers)** reject any ordained ministry. There is no set service and anyone may speak during their meetings, in which they gather together to be inspired by the Holy Spirit.

Research activity 🔍

Using the internet or a library, find out how many members worldwide belong to the Roman Catholic, Orthodox and any three Protestant Churches, and record your findings.

Summary

You should now be able to explain what is meant by the Body of Christ and why the different Christian denominations arose. You should also understand the different positions on matters of faith and practice taken by these denominations.

AQA Examiner's tip

You have to know about the Church as the Body of Christ, but the rest of the material in this topic is background information to show you the relationship between Roman Catholics and other Christians.

Activities

1 Explain what the Church is.
2 Explain the main differences between Orthodox and Catholic Christians.

⚭ links

You can find out about the sacraments, including baptism, in Chapter 2.

Discussion activity ▪▪▪

With a partner or in a small group discuss whether the existence of so many different denominations poses any problems for Christians.

Activities

3 Explain what the Reformation was.
4 Explain why Roman Catholics are so called.

Extension activity

Draw a timeline or family tree to show when and from which denominations the different Christian denominations started.

The role of Peter

Peter and Jesus

For Roman Catholics, the central passage of the Bible about the role of **Peter** is the one at Caesarea Philippi:

Beliefs and teachings

Peter's confession of Christ

When Jesus came to the region of Caesarea Philippi, he asked his disciples, 'Who do people say the Son of Man is?'

They replied, 'Some say John the Baptist; others say Elijah; and still others, Jeremiah or one of the prophets.'

'But what about you?' he asked. 'Who do you say I am?'

Simon Peter answered, 'You are the Christ, the Son of the living God.'

Jesus replied, 'Blessed are you, Simon son of Jonah, for this was not revealed to you by man, but by my Father in heaven. And I tell you that you are Peter, and on this rock I will build my church, and the gates of Hades will not overcome it. I will give you the keys of the kingdom of heaven; whatever you bind on earth will be bound in heaven, and whatever you loose on earth will be loosed in heaven.'

Matthew 16:13–19

Objectives

Examine the role of Peter in the early Church.

Evaluate the character of Peter.

Key terms

Peter: the leading Apostle. Peter was the 'Rock' on which Jesus based the Church and was the first pope.

AQA Examiner's tip

While the incident at Caesarea Philippi is not a set text, so you will not be tested on it, knowing it will give you the basis of any answer about Peter and his role.

The following points are important about this event:

- Peter was the first human to call Jesus the Christ.
- Peter's response was due to God's inspiration.
- Jesus called Simon 'Peter', meaning 'rock'.
- Jesus says that on the rock of Peter, Jesus will build his Church; Peter will be the solid foundation on which other Christians will rely.
- Hell (sin and evil) will not be able to defeat the Church.
- All Peter's decisions will be upheld by the power of heaven.

This incident shows that Jesus was able to see the commitment that Simon had. Jesus knew that other disciples would need a leader, someone who knew the mind of Jesus and who had learned through making mistakes. Jesus appointed Simon the fisherman to be the bedrock of the faith of other followers, the one who would be able to guide them in need, and he named him Peter.

Activities

1. How easy do you think it was for Peter to call Jesus the Christ? Explain your answer.
2. Explain the importance of the promises Jesus made to Peter.

A *Jesus and Peter on the water – stained glass*

Case study

The example of Peter

Vera is a 54-year-old Roman Catholic, a regular churchgoer.

'To my mind Peter is one of the most human of people in the Bible. He is impulsive and usually gets things wrong. When Jesus first called him, he immediately left everything! At Caesarea Philippi, he gave the answer that God inspired him to give, but then he ruined everything by telling Jesus that the Christ could not suffer, showing he misunderstood what Jesus was saying. When Jesus was arrested and taken for trial, Peter was both interested enough and nosey enough to find out what was going on. But as soon as trouble appeared possible, he denied knowing Jesus. Yet through it all Jesus forgave him and gave him another chance to make a mess of things. Peter gives me real hope that my situation isn't hopeless!'

Peter after the Resurrection

When Jesus was on trial Peter denied that he knew him (Mark 14:66–72), but despite this Jesus reinstated him, saying: 'Feed my lambs ... Feed my sheep' (John 21:14–17), i.e. look after my followers.

Following Jesus' command to him, Peter took over the leadership of the early community straight after the Resurrection. The rest of the Apostles looked up to Peter as the successor to Jesus, and always gave his opinion great respect. This is described in Acts chapters 1–6 and 10–12.

According to tradition, Peter was executed in about 67 CE, during Nero's persecution of the Christians following the great fire of Rome. Tradition says that Peter was crucified upside down and that he was buried in the Vatican Hill outside Rome.

B   *Statue of St Peter*

Activities

3   Choose a passage from The Acts of the Apostles that features Peter and explain what it shows about Peter and his role.

4   'Peter had too many weaknesses in his personality to make a good leader.' Do you agree? Give reasons for your answer, showing that you have thought about more than one point of view.

Extension activity

Draw a strip cartoon to illustrate the passage from The Acts of the Apostles that you chose in Activity 3.

Research activity

Look up **three** of the following passages: Mark 8:27–33, Mark 14:26–31, Mark 14:66–72, John 18:1–11, John 20:1–10, John 21:1–23. What do these passages show you about Peter's personality?

Summary

You should now be able to explain why Jesus chose Peter and what Peter's role was in the early Church. You should also have an opinion about whether Peter's character was right for the chosen role.

1.10 The role of the Pope

The Bishop of Rome

Peter is counted as the first Bishop of Rome. The Bishop of Rome is called the Pope. Roman Catholics believe that the promises made by Jesus to Peter have been passed on to all Peter's successors. There has been an unbroken succession of Bishops of Rome, and all have passed on the faith of the Apostles. Benedict XVI was elected in 2005 as the 267th Pope since Peter.

The Vatican

The Pope lives in the Vatican, the smallest independent country in the world. It is centred around St Peter's Basilica. The High (main) Altar of St Peter's is built immediately above the tomb of St Peter. It is a way of stressing the continuation of Christ's promise in the successor to Peter, the current Pope.

Election of a new Pope

When a Pope dies, all the cardinals (leaders in the Church) gather together and are locked away without contact with the outside world until they agree on a new Pope. He must be a male Catholic. The guidance of the Holy Spirit is sought before each ballot, in the hope that each cardinal will be inspired to nominate the person most pleasing to God for the position. The person elected must have a total vote of two-thirds plus one of all the votes, to show there is full support for this election.

Objectives

Examine what the role of the Pope is in relation to the role of Peter.

Explain the relevance of the Pope for Roman Catholics.

Key terms

The Pope: the head of the Roman Catholic Church. The successor of Peter who was appointed to lead the Church by Jesus.

Head of the Church: the Pope is the one who tells all Roman Catholics what they ought to believe; he expresses the opinion of the Church.

Activity

1. Explain why it is important for Roman Catholics that there has been a direct line of succession from St Peter to Pope Benedict XVI.

A *St Peter's Square in the Vatican City*

The Pope as head of the Roman Catholic Church and spiritual guide

The name Peter means 'rock' and the Pope continues to be the solid foundation upon which the faith of the whole community can rely. The whole Church is guided by the Holy Spirit, but this is particularly true of the Pope.

Roman Catholics believe that the Church is infallible, i.e. it cannot go wrong, because it is guided by the Holy Spirit. When the Pope speaks *ex cathedra* (i.e. in his official capacity as **Head of the Church** and the Vicar of Christ on earth), he is infallible in matters of faith – this is called Papal Infallibility.

The Pope regularly issues encyclicals (documents) dealing with important matters of the time. These documents are not infallible but do give Catholics great guidance over important issues.

The Pope represents the spiritual guidance of the whole Church. The Church is 2000 years old and the whole Church community has had a lot of experience dealing with new ideas and suggestions. The guidance offered by the Pope reflects the tradition of the Church, which needs to be treated with respect.

As 'universal pastor' (shepherd of the whole world) the Pope appoints bishops throughout the world.

B   Inside St Peter's Basilica

Activities

2   Explain why the Vatican is important for Roman Catholics.

3   Explain how a Pope is chosen.

AQA   Examiner's tip

If you think of the role of your head, especially your brain, which controls your whole body, you might get some insight into the role of the Pope. He is the one who makes sure the whole body of the Church goes in the right direction.

Activities

4   Explain what is meant by the Pope's 'infallibility'.

5   Why is infallibility important to Roman Catholics?

6   'Roman Catholics do not need to pay attention to what the Pope teaches.' Do you agree? Give reasons for your answer, showing that you have thought about more than one point of view.

Research activity 🔍

Choose one Pope from the 20th century. In what ways did this Pope help Roman Catholics?

Summary

You should now be able to explain what the role of the Pope is, especially as the successor to Peter. You should also be able to support an opinion about the need for the Pope.

Extension activity

Find out about a time of major change in the Church and the role that the Pope played in these changes. You could choose the Reformation, the Counter-Reformation or when the Popes lost control of central Italy in the 19th century.

The Magisterium

Magisterium is a Latin word that refers to the teaching authority of the Church. The Pope and the bishops in the Roman Catholic Church form **the Magisterium** (see pages 26–27). The Pope is the head of the Magisterium. Jesus made it clear to his disciples that for him, authority led to service or ministry. One of the main titles of the Pope, the Head of the Church, is the Servant of the Servants of God. Whenever the Magisterium and the Pope are thought about as having authority, they also have to minister to the needs of the members of the Church. This is known as the **teaching ministry** of the Church.

At the Last Supper Christ promised his disciples: 'When he, the Spirit of truth, comes, he will guide you into all truth' (John 16:13). At Pentecost the Holy Spirit came down on all the disciples and filled them with his power. This Spirit is at work in each member of the Church, but more especially in the Church as a whole. Christians have Jesus' promise that the Church will never go astray even if individuals go wrong.

Down the centuries the whole Church has been involved in the process of understanding the full message of Jesus and applying it to each generation. The truth is unchanging but sometimes the way it is expressed needs to develop.

The Church never pronounces on things on the spur of the moment, nor accepts new ideas quickly. An idea has to pass two basic tests which are:

- the test of time
- the test of how widely accepted it is.

Only when something is almost universally accepted as important to faith will the Church make a formal statement. This is because the Church fears that if it pronounced on something that was then shown to be false, people would stop believing the eternal truths as well. Therefore the Church is very slow to make pronouncements, but when it does they can be accepted as true.

A A bishop's mitre

■ The role of the bishops in the Magisterium

The Pope, as the Bishop of Rome, is helped throughout the world by the **bishops**. They also advise the Pope on local issues. The bishops are the successors to the Apostles, just as the Pope is the successor to St Peter, the leader of the Apostles.

The bishops are appointed by the Pope after consultation with local people. Each bishop is responsible for a particular (usually geographical) area of the Church. The bishop has to report regularly to the Pope on the affairs of the diocese (the area for which the bishop is responsible).

The bishop is the head of the local Church and his main role is to teach the faith in that area. He is responsible for the organisation of the parishes, for the ordination of priests and for the final reception into the Church of new members in confirmation. He often sends out a pastoral letter to the parishes in the diocese, giving information and guidance.

The see (chair or cathedra) of the bishop is a main feature of the cathedral, the central church building of the diocese.

General Councils

Sometimes the Pope can summon all the bishops of the world together to discuss Church affairs. This is called a General Council. The last one was the Second Vatican Council of 1962–1965, which made many changes in the way the Church lived. The most notable of these was changing the Mass from Latin to the language of the local people. At the Councils the voice of the whole Church gathered as one can be heard, but it is always the Pope who has the final say on issues.

B *Liverpool Metropolitan Cathedral of Christ the King*

Discussion activity 👥👥

With a partner or in a small group discuss whether Catholics need bishops or if it is sufficient to have a local priest as a leader.

Research activity 🔍

Find out all you can about your local bishop and what he does in the diocese. Then write a report of your findings.

Activities

4   Explain why bishops are important for the Roman Catholic Church.

5   Explain what a General Council is.

6   'Bishops should be left to run their own dioceses as they want.' Do you agree? Give reasons for your answer, showing that you have thought about more than one point of view.

Summary

You should now be able to explain what the teaching authority of the Church is and what its role is in passing on the Catholic faith. You should also be able to express an opinion on the need for a single teaching authority.

1.12 The impact of the Bible, the Creed and the Magisterium

The Bible

The Bible is the word of God and all Christian teachings must be based on what is contained in the Bible. However, the Bible was written 2000 years ago and needs to be applied to the modern situation. What this means is that people need to take the eternal truths from the Bible and try to live according to these truths. Some of them, such as 'You shall not murder' (Exodus 20:13) and 'Love your neighbour as yourself' (Mark 12:31), are quite obvious guidelines to follow. This does not mean that these principles are easy, just that there is not much doubt about the relevance of them.

It is quite a challenge for many people to be faithful to the central principles put forward in the Bible. This is especially true when there is a great deal of modern pressure to find ways around those parts of the Christian teachings that people feel uncomfortable with. Many people get around this issue simply by saying that the Bible is 2000 years old, so is out of date and can be ignored. Many Roman Catholics look to the Magisterium for guidance about what parts of the Bible should be firmly adhered to today.

Objectives

Understand the effects of the Bible, the Creed and the Magisterium on the believers' lives.

Evaluate the relative importance of these three authorities.

Activity

1 Choose **five** passages from the Bible at random and say, with reasons, how far Christians today should try to live according to the message of each passage.

The Creed

The creeds are the statements of faith that help the believer to know exactly what their religion proclaims. The creeds were drawn up by the bishops as a true statement of the faith, and it is the bishops' responsibility to ensure that the faith found in the creeds is kept pure and complete.

The creeds do not tell people what to do. However, if you believe certain things, this should lead you into certain actions. For instance, if a person accepts that God is the Creator, than the best way to show respect to God is by caring for all creation. This would mean that Christians respect the environment and are concerned about ecological issues. There are many practical effects on the way of life of someone who believes in the teachings of the Creed.

The Magisterium

The Magisterium was responsible for deciding which books were acceptable in the Bible. The Magisterium presents the word of God to the modern world and guides believers as to how best to live by God's guidance. This means that the Bible depends on the teaching authority of the Church, just as much as the teachings of the Church must find their roots in the Bible: the Bible and the Magisterium cannot be separated.

A The Bible

B *The Vatican flag contains the symbol of the Pope: the crossed keys that refer to the keys of heaven that were given to Peter by Jesus (Matthew 16:19)*

Activity

2 Go through each statement of the Apostles' Creed (see page 16 and pages 20–21) and draw up a list of practical things Christians should do as signs that they believe what the Apostles' Creed states.

links

Look back to page 28 to remind yourself that the Magisterium is the teaching authority of the Church.

Tradition is that which is handed on. The Magisterium is responsible for ensuring that that which has lasting truth is preserved so that all believers may feel that they are doing and believing the right things. This means that the teaching authority of the Church cannot come up with anything new; it can only apply eternal truths to new situations. For example, issues connected with reproductive medicine, such as test-tube babies, are not dealt with in the Bible. However, the Magisterium can take central principles from the Bible and apply them to these issues. Because of the experience of the Church in this type of area, believers can have confidence that the guidance is solid and trustworthy.

AQA Examiner's tip

Remember: you have to know more than just what the Bible, the Creed and the Magisterium are. You have to know how they have an impact on the lives of believers.

The Church is unlikely to change its teachings. When the Pope issues an encyclical (document) on modern issues, such as the rights of workers and employers, believers can apply the teachings to their own life with confidence.

Extension activity

Choose one modern problem (medical issues or social issues are best) and examine how the Church has tried to give guidance on this problem, basing its teaching on the principles laid down in the Bible.

Through following what is contained in the Creed and the Bible, interpreted by the teaching authority of the Church, believers can be confident that they are on solid ground in their religious life.

Discussion activity

With a partner or in a small group discuss which of the three – the Bible, the Creed or the Magisterium – is the most important source of authority for Christians today, giving reasons for your opinion.

Activities

3 Explain how the Bible, the Creed and the Magisterium are linked in the passing on of the Christian faith.

4 'Christians only need the Bible for their faith.' Do you agree? Give reasons for your answer, showing that you have thought about more than one point of view.

Summary

You should now be able to explain how the Bible, the Creed and the Magisterium guide believers in their way of life. You should also be able to weigh up opinions about which of these authorities is the most important.

1

Beliefs and sources of authority – summary

For the examination you should now be able to:

✔ know and understand the main beliefs and sources of authority of the Roman Catholic Church

✔ understand differences between Christian groups and individuals in beliefs and interpretation of the Bible

✔ know and understand Christian beliefs as summarised in the Apostles' Creed

✔ describe different kinds of teaching authority and their importance for and contribution to the Roman Catholic way of life

✔ understand the impact of sources of authority on the beliefs and lifestyle of Roman Catholics

✔ appreciate the different arguments about the value of each of these sources of authority.

Sample answer

1 Write an answer to the following exam question.

'A fundamentalist approach is the only proper way to understand the Bible.'

Do you agree? Give reasons for your answer, showing that you have thought about more than one point of view.

(6 marks)

2 Read the following sample answer.

'A fundamentalist approach to the Bible accepts that all the Bible is inspired by God and that there is nothing in the Bible that is not true. This is because God is true and he will not mislead the people who are faithful to him. If people accept this position they will follow what is in the Bible, knowing that it leads them in the way God wants them to go. People will be happy and everybody will do the same

thing. Surely this is a good thing? The problem is there are contradictions in the Bible, for instance Moses allowing divorce and Jesus forbidding it. Both these statements can't be true, so they can't both come from God. I do not think it is possible to accept the fundamentalist approach at all. God has given us our intelligence to make sense of writings. We must not become slaves of one approach, especially one that might be wrong.'

3 With a partner, discuss the sample answer. Do you think there are other things the student could have included in the answer?

4 What mark would you give this answer out of 6? (Look at the mark scheme in the Introduction on page 7 (AO2) before you attempt this.) What are the reasons for the mark you have given?

AQA Examination-style questions

1 Look at the photograph below and answer the following questions.

 AQA Examiner's tip All of the questions below are 6-mark evaluation questions. You must state, with reasons, what your own thoughts are on the issue and also give a different point of view. Simply stating what you think will not gain you any credit on its own – the marks are gained by the support you can give to these views in argument and evidence. If you consider more than one point of view, you will have the opportunity to gain full marks.

(a) Explain what the Apostles' Creed says about Jesus. *(6 marks)*

 AQA Examiner's tip In (a) you have to clearly refer to what the Creed says about Jesus as God and man. You must also make sure you explain the meaning of the statements. If you only write out the correct sections of the Apostles' Creed you are unlikely to gain more than 4 marks out of 6.

(b) 'The Apostles' Creed is no longer relevant for Christians.' Do you agree? Give reasons for your answer, showing that you have thought about more than one point of view. *(6 marks)*

(c) Explain how the Pope and the teaching authority of the Church might help a Roman Catholic. *(6 marks)*

 AQA Examiner's tip In (c) it is not enough to say who the Pope is and what the teaching authority is. You have to show how their teachings can help a Roman Catholic and why.

(d) 'Christians should only follow the teachings of the Bible.' Do you agree? Give reasons for your answer, showing that you have thought about more than one point of view. *(6 marks)*

2.1 The sacraments of the Roman Catholic Church

What is a sacrament?

There are seven **sacraments** in the Roman Catholic Church: baptism, confirmation, the Eucharist, marriage, ordination, reconciliation and the sacrament of the sick.

A sacrament is an outward sign of inward grace ordained by Jesus Christ by which grace is given to the soul.

What this means is that each sacrament not only symbolises the giving of grace by actions and words, but also helps to make what is symbolised a reality for the believer. Grace is the life of God freely given, which increases in the believer every time a sacrament is received. 'Ordained by Jesus Christ' means that the sacrament originates in the work and teaching of Jesus.

Objectives

Examine what is meant by a sacrament.

Understand how sacraments help Christians in their relationship with God.

Key terms

Sacraments: rites and rituals through which the believer receives a special gift of grace. Roman Catholics believe that sacraments are 'outward signs' of 'inward grace'. Different Christian traditions celebrate different sacraments.

A *The actions, words and symbolism/result of the seven sacraments*

Sacrament	Action	Symbolism/result	Words from the Roman Missal
Baptism	the pouring of water	the cleansing of sins	'I baptise you in the name of the Father and of the Son and of the Holy Spirit.'
Confirmation	the anointing of the forehead with chrism (holy oil) and the laying on of hands	receiving the gifts and power of the Holy Spirit	'Be sealed with the gift of the Holy Spirit.'
Eucharist	the receiving of the consecrated bread and wine, the Body and Blood of Christ	receiving the fullness of Christ	'This is my body. This is my blood.'
Marriage	the consent	both partners accepting the other person as husband/wife for life	'Will you, [full name], take [full name] here present as your lawful wedded husband/wife according to the rites of our Holy Mother the Church?' 'I will.'
Ordination	the laying on of hands and the anointing of the hands with chrism	conferring the dignity of the priesthood	'Almighty Father, grant to this servant of yours the dignity of the priesthood.'
Reconciliation	the laying on of hands	the passing on of God's power of forgiveness	'I absolve you from your sins in the name of the Father and of the Son and of the Holy Spirit.'
Sacrament of the sick	the laying on of hands and the anointing of the hands with chrism	strengthening and forgiveness	'Through this holy anointing may the Lord in his love and mercy help you with the grace of the Holy Spirit. May the Lord who frees you from sin save you and raise you up. Amen.'

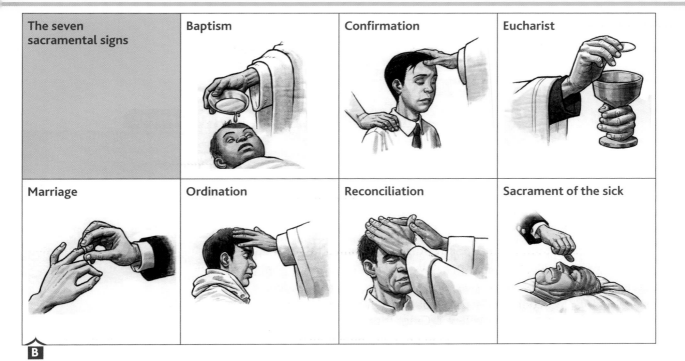

The seven sacramental signs	Baptism	Confirmation	Eucharist
Marriage	Ordination	Reconciliation	Sacrament of the sick

B

Each of the sacraments is seen as a meeting point with God. Christians welcome Christ into their lives at central moments. Each of the sacraments builds up the relationship in a different way:

- In **baptism** a person becomes a child of God.
- In **confirmation** the faith is strengthened and the power of the Holy Spirit is renewed in the believer's life.
- Through the **Eucharist** the life of Christ is received, enabling the believer to continue growing in God's love.
- In **marriage** the couple accept that their love for each other is the love of God active in their lives.
- In **ordination** the priest commits himself to God and to the Church and is given the powers to exercise the priestly office.
- In **reconciliation** the believer rejects those areas of life that have damaged their relationship with God and this relationship is restored.
- In the **sacrament of the sick**, the sick are made aware of the strength and love of Christ with them in their time of need.

The Eucharist, reconciliation and the sacrament of the sick can be received regularly. Baptism, confirmation and ordination can only be received once. Marriage cannot be received a second time while your partner is still alive.

Activities

1 Name the seven sacraments.

2 Write about the central action of each of the seven sacraments.

Research activity

Choose one of the seven sacraments and interview a person who has recently received that sacrament. Ask the person how they felt both before and after receiving the sacrament.

AQA *Examiner's tip*

Make sure that you know what the definition of a sacrament is. For this exam you only have to know about baptism, confirmation and the Eucharist in detail.

Summary

You should now be able to explain what is meant by a sacrament and understand how sacraments help Christians in their relationship with God.

Sacraments as rites of passage and rites of initiation

Rites of passage

A rite is a ceremony, and the term is used especially about the things that are said and done during that particular ceremony. Rites, which often include symbolic actions, are impressive ceremonies that underline the importance of the event celebrated.

For Roman Catholics every stage in life is a growing point, a chance to develop as an individual. Part of this development involves the believers accepting the role of God in their lives. The Church is the community of believers. New members accept their relationships with other people as an expression of their commitment to God and to the Church. Roman Catholics mark each milestone or new stage in life with a special ceremony that has a religious significance. These are called **rites of passage**. There are four major stages in life, and Roman Catholics celebrate each of these stages with a rite of passage:

- **Birth**, the beginning of life, is marked by baptism. This also shows that the baby has entered into the life of the family of God.
- **Maturity**, the taking of responsibility for your own life rather than depending on others such as your parents, is marked by confirmation. This is an acceptance by believers that they are now committed to the faith that they have chosen, and that they are prepared to do something to show this commitment.
- **Marriage** is when two people join together as one in a new, exclusive relationship. The two people commit themselves to each other to face the unknown future together as one.
- **Death** is when this earthly life is over. The believer is committed to the loving care of God in the hope that their soul will live with God for eternity.

With the exception of the death rites, the rites of passage are also sacraments, showing that God is with people at every stage of their lives. More importantly for believers, God is invited into their lives through these rites of passage. These indicate that every life is holy and that all parts of life are holy and should be respected as such. By stressing the religious aspect of these stages of life, believers are saying that there is nothing that is outside God's concern.

Activities

1. Draw a simple diagram to show the different stages in a person's life and the rites of passage associated with each stage.

2. 'It would be better just to have a family party to celebrate each stage of a person's life than to have a rite of passage.' Do you agree? Give reasons for your answer, showing that you have thought about more than one point of view.

Sacraments of initiation

Initiation is an act in which a person is formally admitted into a group. It is a sign of belonging. In Christianity, two of the rites of passage are also rites of initiation.

Through **baptism** (whether received as an infant or as a believer) a person becomes a child of God and a member of God's family, the Church. When baptism is received as an adult the newly baptised are also anointed with chrism (holy oil) to show the power of the Holy Spirit filling their lives.

When baptism is received as an infant, the Roman Catholic Church offers the believer the sacrament of **confirmation** later in life. This makes the believers full members of the Church through personal commitment. It gives them the powers that they need to live this out in all aspects of their lives. Religion is therefore not seen as something extra to life but a fulfilment of what God wants each individual to be.

A *All rites of passage and rites of initiation are holy events*

Summary

You should now be able to explain what is meant by a rite of passage and a rite of initiation. You should understand how rites of passage celebrate different stages of human life, and the importance of initiation for Christians.

Activities

3 Explain the importance of each rite of initiation for Roman Catholics.

4 Explain why having religious celebrations of the different stages of life is thought to be important to Roman Catholics.

Research activity

1 Investigate five different organisations or groups that perform some simple ceremony to welcome new members e.g. the Scouts, Air Cadet Corps, etc. Summarise what happens in these ceremonies. What is the purpose of these ceremonies? Why do people join these groups and in what ways do these groups make the members feel special? Can you see any parallels here with the Christian rites of initiation? Explain your answer.

Research activity

2 Why do many societies celebrate a person's 18th birthday and wedding day? Examine some of the practices that take place on these occasions to make them special. How would you feel if other people ignored these events in your life? Explain your answer. Is there any similarity here to Christian rites of passage? Explain your answer.

The history of baptism

Christian **baptism** goes back to the baptism performed by John the Baptist. John totally submerged people in the river Jordan to show that they wanted to change their lifestyle and turn to God. This was the baptism that Jesus received as recorded in Mark's Gospel in the Bible:

> #### Beliefs and teachings
>
> At that time Jesus came from Nazareth in Galilee and was baptized by John in the Jordan. As Jesus was coming up out of the water, he saw heaven being torn open and the Spirit descending on him like a dove. And a voice came from heaven: 'You are my Son, whom I love; with you I am well pleased.'
>
> *Mark* 1:9–11

For Jesus, this was the start of his ministry, the time when he was publicly dedicated to doing the work of God. However, this baptism was only a sign of people wanting to change their ways. It did not actually remove sins in the way Catholics believe Christian baptism does.

A *The baptism of Jesus – stained glass window*

Objectives

Examine the history of the rite of baptism and confirmation.

Understand why the present separation of baptism and confirmation happened.

Key terms

Baptism: the sacrament through which people become members of the Church. Baptism uses water as a symbol of the washing away of sin. It is a rite of initiation.

Discussion activity

Discuss with a partner or in a small group whether you think Christians should be baptised as Jesus was, giving your reasons.

Activity

1   Why do you think Jesus went to be baptised? How might this help people who are not sure whether they want to be baptised?

After his Resurrection, according to Matthew's Gospel in the Bible, Jesus told his followers:

> ## Beliefs and teachings
>
> 'Therefore go and make disciples of all nations, baptizing them in the name of the Father and of the Son and of the Holy Spirit, and teaching them to obey everything I have commanded you. And surely I am with you always, to the very end of the age.'
>
> *Matthew* 28:19–20

> ### AQA Examiner's tip
>
> It is worth knowing the two passages from the Bible as they will help you with evaluation answers. However, you will not be asked a direct question about these passages.

From that time on, being baptised has been the sign of a person accepting Jesus as their Lord and Saviour.

In the early Church (for the first 300 years), being a Christian could lead to a horrific death. As a result only mature people were baptised. During the Easter Vigil service (see pages 134–135), the converts would be taken by a priest to a place of running water and baptised. Then the newly baptised would be clothed in a white garment and brought to the bishop. He would give them the gift of the Holy Spirit by the laying on of hands. Finally they would join in the Eucharist for the first time. In this way, a person would become a full Christian. This practice shows how the three sacraments of baptism, confirmation and the Eucharist together make a person a full Christian.

> ### Activity
>
> 2   Explain what happened at a baptism ceremony in the early Church.

When it was no longer illegal to be a Christian and the persecutions ended, many people became Christians. Two different developments had an effect on Christian practices of initiation:

1   So many people were being baptised, especially the very young, that it became impossible for a bishop to attend every baptism. It was also not possible for baptisms just to be done at the Easter Vigil, so the laying on of hands became the separate ceremony of confirmation (see pages 52–53).

2   People believed that a person could not go to heaven if they had not been baptised. Many young children died at this time through disease, and parents were worried what would happen to them after death. Therefore, they started baptising infants, often as soon as they were born. This was to ensure that the children went to heaven if they died young.

> ### Research activity 🔍
>
> Research how adults are now received into the Roman Catholic Church at Easter.

> ### Extension activity
>
> Find and examine five different texts from the New Testament that deal with baptism and say how important you think each text is for Christians today.

> ## Activities
>
> 3   Explain why the two passages from the Bible shown above are important for Christian baptism.
>
> 4   Explain why Christians moved from baptising only adults to the practice of baptising infants.
>
> 5   'It would be better if the Roman Catholic rites of initiation went back to the form used by the early Christians.' Do you agree? Give reasons for your answer, showing that you have thought about more than one point of view.

> ### Summary
>
> You should now be able to explain how the rite of baptism and confirmation originated, and why the two parts were later separated into two different rites.

2.4　The rites of baptism

As with all ceremonies or rites in the Roman Catholic Church, there is a set order of words and actions for receiving baptism. Most Roman Catholics receive baptism when they are infants, so the most common form of the ceremony is the rite of infant baptism. However, there is a slightly different form for the baptism of adults. This is also given below, highlighting the points of difference between the two ceremonies. The symbolism of both ceremonies is the same.

The rite of infant baptism

The following is the most common ceremony used:

- The parents, godparents and child are met at the door to the church. The priest greets the parents and godparents and they ask for the child to be baptised.
- The priest makes the sign of the cross on the child.
- The priest reads out passages from the Bible that show the importance of baptism. This is followed by Bidding Prayers, which are a series of short prayers asking God to protect the baby, the parents and the Church community.
- The priest says a prayer that casts out the power of evil. This is because Roman Catholics believe that everybody is born with original sin (best thought of as the tendency to be attracted to doing the wrong thing). Before a person becomes a child of God, this power of evil is removed and replaced by the power of God. Original sin is removed at the moment of baptism.
- The priest anoints the child with an oil of strength (called the oil of catechumens).
- The priest blesses the baptismal water.
- The parents and godparents reject Satan and the power of sin, and state their faith in God the Father, Son and Spirit and in the Catholic Church. Note that here the parents and godparents renew their own faith, the faith that they wish to share with the child.

A　A baby being baptised

Objectives

Examine the rites of baptism.

AQA　Examiner's tip

For the exam you have to know the rite of infant baptism. You might be able to remember it more easily by bullet-pointing it in your exercise books.

Beliefs and teachings

Introduction to the baptismal vows

'Dear parents and God-parents. You have come here to present this child for baptism. By water and the Holy Spirit she/he is to receive the gift of new life from God, who is love. On your part, you must make it your constant care to bring her/him up in the practice of the faith. See that the divine life which God gives her/him is kept safe from the poison of sin, to grow always stronger in his heart.'

From the Rite of Infant Baptism, **Roman Missal**

Research activity

1　Interview people who are godparents and ask them about the ceremony, including their own renewal of baptismal vows, and their role as godparents in the baby's life.

⚭links

The meaning and symbolism of each of these elements in the ceremony are explained on pages 42–43.

- The priest pours water over the child's head while saying: 'I baptise you in the name of the Father, and of the Son and of the Holy Spirit.' (This is the actual moment of baptism.)
- The priest anoints the child with chrism (holy oil).
- The priest gives the child a white garment.
- The priest gives the child a candle lit from the Paschal (Easter) candle.
- The priest prays over the child's ears and mouth so that the child may hear God's word and praise God.
- All say the Our Father (see pages 94–95), after which the priest says the blessing for the child, for the parents and for the whole community.

The baptism of older people

If an older person is baptised, the main differences are as follows:

- The person speaks the vows for themselves, though a sponsor (instead of godparents) is still present. A sponsor is a confirmed Catholic who agrees to support the newly baptised Christian on the spiritual journey.
- The anointing with chrism is often replaced by the conferring of the Holy Spirit. This goes back to the practice of the early Church (see page 39), when the new member received the Holy Spirit by the laying on of hands and the anointing at the same ceremony.
- Mass follows, and the newly baptised receives Holy Communion for the first time, making him or her a full member of the Church.

Activities

1 Either act out with a partner, or do a series of drawings, to show the stages of a rite of infant baptism.

2 'A Christian only needs to be baptised to be a follower of Jesus.' Do you agree? Give reasons for your answer, showing that you have thought about more than one point of view.

B *A baptismal font*

Summary

You should now be able to describe the stages of the rite of baptism, for either infants or older people who wish to be baptised as Catholics.

∞ links

You can find out about Holy Communion in Chapter 5.

Discussion activity

Discuss with a partner or in a small group whether you think the baptismal vows are important in the rite of infant baptism, giving your reasons.

Research activity

2 There are times when it is not possible for the whole rite of baptism to take place. Give an example of a situation when this might be the case. Examine what parts of the rite have to be performed. Who can baptise? In what circumstances can someone else replace a priest? Design a short leaflet explaining to other Christians why they need to know what to do at a baptism.

Research activity

3 Interview a person who has been or who is about to be baptised as a Roman Catholic as an older person. Discuss how they felt about the preparations that took place before baptism. How did they feel about the moment of baptism? Do they think that it would be better for adults to be fully immersed in water or to have water poured on their head?

Extension activity

Find out all you can about original sin. Why is this idea important for Roman Catholics? How has this idea affected the development and understanding of the sacrament of baptism?

2.5 The meaning, purpose and symbolism of baptism

The meaning and purpose of baptism

Baptism is the only sacrament that is accepted by nearly all Christian groups. The few exceptions include the Salvation Army and the Quakers, who do not think that a rite or ceremony is needed.

Baptism is accepted by Christians as long as it is performed by a baptised Christian. All that is needed for a Christian to baptise another person is for water to be poured on the head as the baptiser says: 'I baptise you in the name of the Father, and of the Son and of the Holy Spirit.'

Baptism can only be received once. It is the sign of becoming a member of the Christian community, a sign of initiation (of belonging).

Being baptised in water symbolises accepting the teaching of Jesus and wanting to follow him into eternal life. By entering 'the waters of the tomb' the Christian signals the death of their old self and rising to new life in Christ.

Consequently baptism should be a turning point in a person's life. It should mark a rejection of sin and all that separates the person from God, and a striving to live a life of perfection following the teaching and example of Jesus.

Through baptism believers have all their sins, including original sin (see page 40), removed so they are able to live their life in a strong relationship with God. The separation from God that is the result of sin is removed in baptism.

Through baptism a believer becomes a son or daughter of God, a relationship that should be built upon throughout the person's life. At the same time the believer becomes a member of the Body of Christ, the Church community. The Church is there to support the individual throughout life.

Once people have received baptism they may receive all the other sacraments. According to the Catholic Church a person who is not baptised cannot receive the other sacraments.

The symbolism of baptism

The ceremony of baptism is full of symbols, each of which stresses some aspect of the meaning of baptism. These symbols, in the order in which they appear in the ceremony, are explained in Table **A**.

Objectives

Examine what baptism means for believers.

Understand how the symbols used in baptism bring out the purpose of the sacrament.

Evaluate the importance of the meanings and purposes of baptism.

 links

You can find out more about the Quakers on page 66, and about the Salvation Army and the Quakers on pages 23 and 120–121.

Discussion activity

Discuss with a partner or in a small group whether you think the idea of 'the waters of the tomb' has any meaning for Christians today, giving your reasons.

Activities

1. Which **three** of the meanings or purposes of baptism do you think are the most important? Explain your answer.

2. When do you think a Christian might feel called upon to baptise someone? Use examples in your answer.

A *The symbols of baptism and their meaning*

Symbol	Meaning
Being met at the door of the church	The person is being welcomed into the Church community.
Sign of the cross	The person now belongs to Christ – it is like the old brand mark to show to whom a slave belonged.
Bible readings	God is present in his guidance and in his word.
Casting out evil	The power of evil is driven away so that the person may be filled with God's grace.
Anointing with the oil of catechumens	This is the giving of strength to fight off the attraction of evil.
Baptismal water	Water is a sign of life (it is needed for survival) and of death (drowning, as in Noah's flood, and the drowning of the Egyptians in the Sea of Reeds when they pursued the Jews).
Pouring of water or immersion in water	The person joins Christ in the tomb of death and rises with him to new life. Sin is washed away.
Anointing with chrism	The person is a prophet (sent to tell others about Christ), a priest (offering God praise) and a king (heir to the Kingdom of Heaven).
White garment	This shows the purity of the soul now that sin has been removed, and a challenge to keep the soul pure for eternal life.
Lighted candle	This is the light of the Risen Christ that the person should carry with them throughout life.
Prayer over the mouth and ears	The person should hear and proclaim God's praise.

B *Some symbols used in baptism*

Activity

3 'There are too many different parts to the rite of infant baptism. They are not all needed'. Do you agree? Give reasons for your answer, showing that you have thought about more than one point of view.

Activities

4 Choose four of the symbols used in baptism. Explain what each symbolises and how it is used.

5 'Every symbol used in the rite of baptism is important.' Do you agree? Give reasons for your answer, showing that you have thought about more than one point of view.

AQA Examiner's tip

To appreciate the full meaning of baptism, learn the meaning of the symbols.

Summary

You should now be able to explain what baptism means for believers and understand how the symbols used in baptism bring out the purpose of the sacrament. You should also be able to evaluate the importance of the meanings and purposes of baptism.

Infant baptism and the impact of baptism on a believer

The practice of infant baptism

When a child is born its parents want to share all that is good with the baby. Parents who have a strong faith will want to help their child grow up in a knowledge and love of God. Catholics believe that **infant baptism**, where the child is initiated into the Church at an early age, is the best way for this to happen. In baptism a child becomes a son or daughter of God and is given the Holy Spirit to guide them.

As a part of a believing community, a child can grow up surrounded by people who care for them and want to share their faith with them. A simple example of this is the commitment of the Roman Catholic Church in England and Wales to ensure that there are primary and secondary Catholic schools for members of the Church.

A *Parents want what is best for their baby, including baptism*

When people are freed from the effects of original sin, which happens in baptism, they are better able to resist the temptation to do wrong. This means that they can live a more sinless life and end up happier.

Some people feel that an individual should be allowed to make a deliberate choice later in life. However, human nature is such that unless a person has a 'feel' for what is available, they will not make a deliberate choice for God – it is easier to reject something than it is to accept it.

The impact of baptism on a believer

All the sacraments have an effect on a believer's life. Sometimes people go through the ceremony of the sacrament but fail to follow through its meaning in their lives. This applies quite a lot to baptism as many people get their child (or themselves) 'done' simply to do what is expected. They do not do it because they really believe in the commitment they are taking on. Roman Catholics teach that the baptism itself takes effect even if the person who is baptised is unaware of or ignores the meaning of the ceremony for a long time. God's grace is available when the person decides to turn to it. In some ways it is like having a million pounds in the bank but never touching it or gaining any interest on it. God's gift is there, waiting to be used.

What difference should baptism make to a believer?

All Christians are called upon to bear witness to God and Christ in their lives, always remembering that actions speak louder than words. Specifically, this means the following:

- A baptised Christian has made a commitment to follow the teachings of Jesus and to build up a relationship with God in prayer.
- This should create a more positive attitude towards other people and towards life, as well as ensuring that time is given to God on a regular basis.
- A Christian needs to take part in the Church activities as far as their age allows.
- It is important for a Christian to remember that it is not 'I was baptised' but 'I am baptised', i.e. baptism is an ongoing living event in the life of the Christian.
- By living according to the teachings of Jesus and the Church, the believer can gain a better understanding of the fullness of life.

Activities

3   What differences should baptism make to the way people lead their lives?

4   'Babies cannot make a commitment so they should not be baptised.' Do you agree? Give reasons for your answer, showing that you have thought about more than one point of view.

AQA   Examiner's tip

Look at the arguments on both sides without allowing yourself to form your own opinion too soon, as you might miss essential arguments.

Extension activity

Research five different Christian denominations' attitudes towards the practice of infant baptism.

Case study

A proper reason for baptism?

Rita and Sean got married in church to please her parents, who are regular churchgoers. Apart from their marriage, neither Rita nor Sean has been inside a church. Rita's parents want their grandson, Philip, to be baptised and are prepared to do what they can to take Philip to church. The local Roman Catholic school is the best school in the area. Rita and Sean decide to have their baby baptised.

Discussion activity ●●●

Discuss with a partner or in a small group whether, if you were the local Roman Catholic priest, you would baptise Philip. Explain your answer.

Summary

You should now understand why infants are baptised and be able to explain the effects of baptism in a believer's life. You should also have an opinion about the importance of infant baptism.

Believers' baptism

Why is believers' baptism practised?

Some Christian denominations choose to baptise people as adults, when they themselves can confirm that they believe in the Christian faith.

Baptist and Pentecostal churches use believers' baptism. A Pentecostal church is a Christian community that centres its approach on the events of the first Pentecost when the Apostles received the Holy Spirit (see page 48). These groups believe that baptism is an outward sign of inner conversion that can only happen after a process of thought and prayer. Therefore it is important to have knowingly accepted Jesus as a personal saviour before accepting baptism.

Believers' baptism involves total immersion in water. This is because those who practise it claim that, since Jesus was baptised as an adult by total immersion, this is the best way to be baptised. It also ensures that the individual personally understands the Christian faith to which they are committing themselves.

Once the commitment is made, the baptised person is expected to play an active role in the life of the Christian community, bearing witness to their belief.

Objectives

Examine what takes place at a believers' baptism.

Assess the impact of believers' baptism on the individual and the community.

Evaluate whether believers' baptism is the best approach to Christian initiation.

Key terms

Believers' baptism: initiation into the Church, by immersion in water, of people old enough to understand the ceremony/rite and willing to live a Christian life. Some denominations prefer this to infant baptism.

⃝⃝ links

The term liturgical is covered in more detail on page 86, or you can look it up in the Glossary at the back of this book.

A An ancient bapistery

The rite of believers' baptism

As believers' baptism is practised mostly in non-liturgical churches, there is no strict form of baptism. However, the following stages tend to occur in most rites of believers' baptism:

- The minister gives a sermon (talk) explaining the importance of baptism and of changing the believer's way of life.
- Those who wish to be baptised are called forward. They sometimes wear light or white clothing as a sign of forgiveness and new life.
- The candidates are asked if they have repented of their sins and have faith in Jesus Christ.

- Each candidate may read a short passage from scripture and give a brief account of how they accepted Jesus as their Lord. This is sometimes called a testimony.

- The minister and the candidate step into a pool (the baptistery) or running water. The minister will say, '[Name] because you have repented of your sins and have requested baptism, I now baptise you in the name of the Father, and of the Son and of the Holy Spirit. Amen.' The candidate is then immersed fully in the water, a sign of the death of their old life.

- The candidate leaves the pool, having risen to new life with Jesus. They then change their clothes before rejoining the service.

Arguments in favour of believers' baptism rather than infant baptism

- The person being baptised is fully aware of what is happening.
- The person has a full, conscious, free choice in the matter.
- The newly baptised can make an instant commitment to living fully the Christian life, including teaching others about Christ.
- Believers' baptism is publicly affirming what the person believes. Through this event, believers commit themselves to following the example of Christ fully, to live a new life in Christ and in the Christian community.
- It takes place when the person wants it to happen, regardless of how old they are.
- Believers' baptism follows the example of Jesus and the early Christians.

B   *Believers being baptised in the river Jordan in the Holy Land*

 Examiner's tip

The best way to understand the arguments about believers' baptism is to compare them with the arguments about infant baptism (see page 44).

Discussion activity

Steve has regularly gone to the local Baptist chapel for the last year. He is 12 years old and wants to be baptised. Do you think Steve is old enough to be baptised as a believer? Discuss the question with a partner or in a small group, giving reasons for your opinion.

Activities

1. Explain why some Christians prefer believers' baptism to infant baptism.
2. Either act out with a partner, or draw a series of pictures, to show what might happen during a rite of believers' baptism.
3. 'Believers' baptism is the only way Christians should be baptised.' Do you agree? Give reasons for your answer, showing that you have thought about more than one point of view.

Summary

You should now be able to explain what takes place at a believers' baptism, and understand the impact of believers' baptism on the individual and the community. You should also have an opinion about whether believers' baptism is the best form of baptism for a Christian.

The origins of confirmation

Before his death, Jesus promised his disciples that he would send them the Holy Spirit:

Beliefs and teachings

'But when he, the Spirit of truth, comes, he will guide you into all truth. He will not speak on his own; he will speak only what he hears, and he will tell you what is yet to come.'

John 16:13

When Jesus appeared to his disciples after the Resurrection:

Beliefs and teachings

Again Jesus said, 'Peace be with you! As the Father has sent me, I am sending you.' And with that he breathed on them and said, 'Receive the Holy Spirit. If you forgive anyone his sins, they are forgiven; if you do not forgive them, they are not forgiven.'

John 20:21–23

After Jesus ascended into heaven the disciples met in prayer regularly. It was during one of these sessions together that they were filled with the Holy Spirit. The Holy Spirit gave the Apostles the confidence to go out and preach about Jesus as Lord. It also gave them the gifts of talking in tongues and healing. Talking in tongues is allowing the Holy Spirit to speak through the person, even though the person does not know the language that is being used.

Beliefs and teachings

The day of Pentecost

When the day of Pentecost came, they were all together in one place. Suddenly a sound like the blowing of a violent wind came from heaven and filled the whole house where they were sitting. They saw what seemed to be tongues of fire that separated and came to rest on each of them. All of them were filled with the Holy Spirit and began to speak in other tongues as the Spirit enabled them.

Acts 2:1–4

When the disciples accepted a person into membership of the Church, the person received the gift of the Holy Spirit. This is the early version of what became the sacrament of **confirmation**.

Beliefs and teachings

When the apostles in Jerusalem heard that [the people of] Samaria had accepted the word of God, they sent Peter and John to them. When they arrived, they prayed for them that they might receive the Holy Spirit, because the Holy Spirit had not yet come upon any of them; they had simply been baptized into the name of the Lord Jesus. Then Peter and John placed their hands on them, and they received the Holy Spirit.

Acts 8:14–17

Objectives

Examine what is meant by confirmation and how the sacrament began.

Understand how confirmation is seen as a rite of initiation.

Evaluate the role of confirmation as a rite of initiation.

∞ links

Look back to pages 10 and 17 for an explanation of what is meant by the Holy Spirit.

AQA Examiner's tip

The passage from Acts 2 about the day of Pentecost is central to understanding the changes made by the Holy Spirit. It is worth studying this short text.

∞ links

You can find out about the festival of Pentecost on pages 136–137.

Key terms

Confirmation: the sacrament in which the faith of the believer is 'confirmed' or strengthened by the Holy Spirit. Those being confirmed personally confirm their acceptance of the promises made by others at their baptism.

Activity

1 What do these passages show about the Holy Spirit?

A *The Holy Spirit is often pictured as a dove*

Activity

2 Why do you think that the Holy Spirit is often pictured as a dove?

Research activity

The gifts of the Spirit received at Pentecost are called charisms. Find out about one Christian group that uses these charisms (e.g. charismatic worshippers).

The history of confirmation

In the early Church, after new believers had been baptised by a priest at the Easter Vigil (see pages 134–135), they were taken into the assembly and presented to the bishop, the leader of the local Church. The bishop would lay his hands on the newly baptised and they would receive the gift of the Holy Spirit. Immediately they would join in celebrating the Eucharist and would receive the Body (bread) and Blood (wine) of Christ for the first time as full members of the Church.

When infant baptism became the normal practice, the bishops, as head of the local Church, wanted to be involved in receiving all new members into the Church. As a result the laying on of hands was removed and became a separate ceremony in the Roman Catholic tradition. Roman Catholics did not receive Holy Communion until they had been confirmed.

In 1907, Pope St Pius X allowed children from the age of seven to receive Holy Communion. Confirmation became more a sacrament of accepting God and the Church, reinforcing what was done on the child's behalf at baptism.

Discussion activity ■■■

Discuss with a partner or in a small group whether you think confirmation should be received at the same time as baptism, giving your reasons.

Activities

3 Explain fully why Communion is often only received once a person has been confirmed.

4 'Baptism is enough. Christians do not need to be confirmed.' Do you agree? Give reasons for your answer, showing that you have thought about more than one point of view.

B *Confirmation candidates are often given religious items as presents*

Summary

You should now be able to explain what is meant by confirmation and how the sacrament began. You should also be able to understand and evaluate the role of confirmation as a rite of initiation.

Confirmation: different practices

In the early Church, baptism, the laying on of hands and the Eucharist were received at one ceremony in that order. This event made a person a full Christian. Since infant baptism became common practice among Christians, the administration of the laying on of hands and the anointing with chrism had tended to become a separate ceremony. Different Christian denominations and different areas have different views as to when this rite should be received, and their practices vary accordingly.

The Orthodox Church

In the Orthodox Church, once a baby is baptised, it is anointed on the head, chest hands and feet with chrism. It also receives Holy Communion at the same ceremony thereby following the order of the sacraments in the early Church. This makes the child a full member of the Church. However, some people question whether it is desirable to administer all the sacraments of initiation at once in such a way that the person never gets the opportunity to accept the faith for themselves.

Different Roman Catholic practices

In some Roman Catholic dioceses, notably Salford, confirmation is received when the children are 7 years old. Many people question whether these children are actually fully aware of what they are taking on. These people argue that the children receive confirmation just because they are told to do so, with no personal choice or commitment. The argument put forward in favour of this age is that the children only receive their first Holy Communion after they have received confirmation, and that this gets back to the original order of the sacraments.

A   *Are these girls old enough to receive confirmation?*

B *Confirmation candidates with the Bishop*

Some dioceses encourage children to receive confirmation when they are 11 years old. At this stage, it is argued, they have some understanding of what is happening and some freedom of choice in the matter. It also allows the children to have the gifts of the Holy Spirit to face the upheavals of puberty and of new schools. Some people would question how free children are at this age and also how much knowledge of their religion and of the Holy Spirit the children would have.

Many Roman Catholic dioceses accept teenagers for confirmation, usually about the age of 15. They have already received their first Holy Communion when they were 7 years old. Now they are given an opportunity to choose for themselves whether they want to be confirmed. Quite a number of teenagers do not choose to be confirmed at this stage, but there is nothing to prevent them from receiving the sacrament when they are ready to do so. Some people would question whether even at this age teenagers are able to make their own choices. Many seem to go along with the majority opinion either to be confirmed or not to be confirmed, rather than making a personal choice.

Some people would argue that 20 years or older is the best age to receive confirmation. There is no question here about the knowledge and the freedom issues. Some people would question whether it is right to deny teenagers the guidance and gifts of the Holy Spirit that can be obtained through the sacrament of confirmation at such an important stage of their development.

The Anglican, Methodist and United Reformed Churches

In the Anglican, Methodist and United Reformed Churches, babies may be baptised but only young adults (or older people) are confirmed. It is usual for people to receive Communion in these churches after they have been confirmed or received into membership.

Summary

You should now know the different ages at which people can be confirmed. You should also understand and be able to evaluate the arguments about these different ages.

Research activity

2 Find out about the practices surrounding confirmation in two other Christian Churches not mentioned on these pages.

∞ links

You can read about the gifts of the Holy Spirit on pages 54–55.

Extension activity

Look on the internet about countries where Christians are persecuted for their faith. Find out what Christians in these countries do about confirmation, especially the age at which confirmation is received. Does this information influence your opinion about confirmation in the UK? Explain your answer.

Activities

1 Draw up a chart that summarises the arguments for and against each age suggested for confirmation.

2 'Confirmation should be received as soon as believers are aware of what they are doing.' Do you agree? Give reasons for your answer, showing that you have thought about more than one point of view.

2.10 Confirmation: the ceremony and symbolism

Preparation for confirmation

Before teenagers are accepted for confirmation, they have to give proof that they are committed. Normally parishes run a short preparation programme that informs the young people about the Holy Spirit and the gifts. Also there are chances to receive the sacrament of reconciliation to be spiritually ready by having sins forgiven.

The ceremony of confirmation

The rite usually takes place during a Mass.

- After the Gospel reading, the candidates are presented to the bishop, who addresses them in the homily (short sermon).
- The candidates renew their baptismal vows.
- The candidates kneel together while the bishop stretches his hands over their heads (the laying on of hands). The bishop says a prayer calling down the power of the Holy Spirit.
- The candidates individually approach the bishop with their sponsor. The sponsor is a confirmed Catholic who is there to support the person being confirmed as an individual. The sponsor also represents the support that the Church community is providing for the confirmation candidates. The sponsor puts his or her hand on the candidate's shoulder.
- The bishop puts his hand on the candidate's head, makes the sign of the cross with chrism on the candidate's forehead and says: '[Name] be sealed with the gift of the Holy Spirit.' The candidate accepts the gift with the word 'Amen'. (This is the actual moment of confirmation.)
- The candidate and the bishop exchange a sign of peace. This is usually a handshake to show that the candidate and the bishop are united in the peace of Christ.

Mass continues with the Bidding Prayers, a series of short prayers that ask God to care for the needs of the Church, the world and individuals.

A *A person being confirmed*

Objectives

Examine the ceremony of confirmation.

Explain the relevance of the symbols used in confirmation.

Evaluate the need for a ceremony of confirmation.

∞ links

For the words of the prayer calling down the power of the Holy Spirit, see page 54.

AQA Examiner's tip

You must know the actions of laying on of hands and anointing with chrism and the words said at this point, because without these exact words and actions there is no sacrament.

Research activity

Find examples of Bidding Prayers and make up some similar prayers of your own.

Activities

1. Either act out with a partner, or draw a strip cartoon, to show the different stages of a ceremony of confirmation.
2. Explain the importance of each part of the ceremony of confirmation.

The symbolism of the ceremony of confirmation

There are many symbols used during the rite of confirmation. Each symbol shows something important about the sacrament.

B *The symbols of the ceremony of confirmation*

Symbol	What it represents
Red vestments	The flame of the Holy Spirit that came on the Apostles at Pentecost.
The bishop	The head of the local Church; he is there to receive people into full membership of the Church.
Renewal of baptismal vows	That the Christians now accept for themselves the faith that was proclaimed on their behalf when they were babies.
Laying on of hands	The passing on of the power of the Holy Spirit.
The sponsor	The support that the local Church community gives to this new member.
Chrism	That the candidate has been set aside for a task and has been chosen by God.
New name chosen by candidate	That the candidate is taking responsibility for themselves, a new stage is reached in their life and they are asking the saint of that name to support and pray for them.
Sign of peace	A sign of unity, shared with the whole Christian community, represented by the bishop.

Case study

Patrick

Patrick is 16 years old and only goes to church when he stays with his grandmother in Ireland. His grandmother has heard that confirmation for those in Patrick's year at school is happening next month. She has gone to great expense to buy an airline ticket and to get time off work to be present when Patrick is confirmed. Patrick is not really bothered about religion and does not want to go to church as his mates might start making fun of him. However, he does not want to disappoint his grandmother.

Discussion activity

With a partner or in a small group, discuss what Patrick should do. Give reasons for your opinion.

Activities

3 Choose the three symbols that you think are the most important in confirmation. Explain your choice.

4 'Christians do not need to be confirmed to accept their faith.' Do you agree? Give reasons for your answer, showing that you have thought about more than one point of view.

Extension activity

Imagine that you have been asked to run a confirmation preparation programme in your parish. You have to explain to the candidates what happens both in theory and in practice in the ceremony of confirmation. How would you plan to give this information and why?

Summary

You should now be able to describe what happens during the ceremony of confirmation and explain the relevance of the symbols used. You should also be able to express an opinion about the need for a ceremony of confirmation.

The gifts of the Holy Spirit

According to Roman Catholic teaching, the Holy Spirit is the power of God at work in the world in the hearts of all people who believe, to help them live a life following God's will and becoming closer to God. The seven **gifts of the Holy Spirit** are:

- wisdom
- understanding
- right judgement (or counsel)
- courage (or fortitude)
- knowledge
- reverence (or piety)
- wonder and awe (or fear of the Lord).

During the confirmation service the bishop stretches his hands over those who are to be confirmed and says the prayer for the outpouring of the Holy Spirit:

> #### Beliefs and teachings
>
> Send your Holy Spirit upon them to be their Helper and Guide.
> Give them the spirit of wisdom and understanding,
> the spirit of right judgement and courage,
> the spirit of knowledge and reverence.
> Fill them with the spirit of wonder and awe in your presence.
>
> *Roman Missal*

These gifts overlap and reinforce each other, but the main idea is that they help the individual to become a full human being.

A The gifts of the Holy Spirit

B A confirmation card

Objectives

Examine what are the gifts of the Holy Spirit.

Explain the relevance of the gifts of the Holy Spirit for Christians.

Evaluate how much Christians need the gifts of the Holy Spirit.

Key terms

Gifts of the Holy Spirit: seven gifts which the Holy Spirit gives to the newly confirmed to help them live full Christian lives. They are wisdom, understanding, right judgement, courage, knowledge, reverence, and wonder and awe.

AQA Examiner's tip

Make sure you know what the gifts of the Spirit are and that you understand how they help Christians live their lives.

The gifts and their effects

- **Wisdom**: This is more than just knowing facts. Wisdom is the ability to appreciate the underlying truths that make the plain facts important. It is the ability to see what certain actions might lead to if followed through.

- **Understanding**: This is more than just appreciating the depth of a piece of information. It has a lot in common with the idea of sympathy and empathy. It is the ability to share deeply in someone else's situation and to appreciate why your own situation is as it is.

- **Right judgement** (or **counsel**): This is the ability to guide another person in the best course of action or the best approach to take in a particular situation. This follows on from the correct use of the gifts of wisdom and understanding.

- **Courage** (or **fortitude**): This is more than the ability to stand up and face an extreme situation (though that is certainly included in this gift); it is the ability to carry on when things are difficult or boring, and to stand up for what is right even though you are the only person taking that stand.

- **Knowledge**: This is more than an awareness of simple facts. It is the awareness of what makes these facts important and how they relate to each other.

- **Reverence** (or **piety**): This is to do with the way people respond to God by living holy lives, showing that God is the centre of all their actions and their approach to each situation.

- **Wonder and awe** (or **fear of the Lord**): This gift is about holding God in the correct esteem – neither being too frightened to approach him because God is too holy nor being so casual in dealing with God that his greatness is undervalued.

Case study

Using the gifts of the Holy Spirit

Phil runs a youth club in his local parish that has been going fairly successfully for two years. Recently, a group of seven young men and three girls have started to come in the middle of the night, some of them slightly drunk at times. Phil wants to help this group to become a part of the whole club as he feels that they need the help and support that the other members could give them. However, he is scared that the group could do more harm than good if they do not respond positively. Phil has to use all the gifts of the Holy Spirit to help him handle the situation. He knows that he needs to show understanding both to the group and to the other members. He has to have the wisdom to know where to draw the lines between acceptable and non-acceptable behaviour. He needs the knowledge of how the different groups interact to help him create the situations that will make the exercise successful.

Summary

You should now be able to explain what the seven gifts of the Holy Spirit are, and to explain and evaluate their relevance for Christians.

Activities

1   Why are the seven gifts of the Holy Spirit important for Roman Catholics?

2   Choose **three** of the gifts of the Holy Spirit. Describe a situation in which each of these gifts might be used. (You may use a different situation for each gift if you want, but you might find that more than one gift can be used in one situation.)

Research activity

Look up 1 Corinthians 12:4–11 in the Bible. What does Paul say about the gifts of the Spirit and how they should be used? Do you think Paul's advice is helpful for Christians today? Explain your answer.

Extension activity

Research the twelve fruits of the Holy Spirit. Show how the correct use of the seven gifts of the Holy Spirit can produce these fruits.

Discussion activities

1   Do you think that Phil is being realistic in his hopes? Discuss with a partner or in a small group, explaining your opinion.

2   With a partner or in a small group, discuss the following statement: 'Christians can live full lives without receiving the gifts of the Holy Spirit.' Give reasons for your opinion.

2

Sacraments of initiation – summary

For the examination you should now be able to:

- ✓ understand what is meant by sacraments of initiation
- ✓ understand the different practices of baptism, the purpose, importance and symbolism of these ceremonies and their impact on the life of the believer
- ✓ understand why some denominations prefer believers' baptism to infant baptism
- ✓ describe ceremonies in detail, paying attention to what is said and done
- ✓ understand the process of initiation and significance of being a committed member of the Roman Catholic Church
- ✓ know of different Christian practices of the sacrament of confirmation, the symbolism, purpose and impact of the sacrament
- ✓ know and understand the gifts of the Holy Spirit in the Roman Catholic tradition.

Sample answer

1 Write an answer to the following exam question:

Explain what happens during a ceremony of believers' baptism.

(6 marks)

2 Read the following sample answer:

The adult who wants to be baptised is met at the door to the church with his godparents and asked what he wants. He asks for baptism and is then led inside the church. There is a reading from the gospel and the new believer says how he started to believe in Jesus. He is then led into a pool of water and the priest says:

'I baptise you in the name of Jesus' as he dunks the new believer totally under the water. The new Christian is then given a lighted candle and is anointed with chrism. Mass then continues as normal.

3 With a partner, discuss the sample answer. Do you think there are other things that the student could have included in the answer?

4 What mark would you give this answer out of 6? (Look at the mark scheme in the Introduction on page 7 (AO1) before you attempt this.) What are the reasons for the mark you have given?

AQA Examination-style questions

1   Look at the photograph below and answer the following questions.

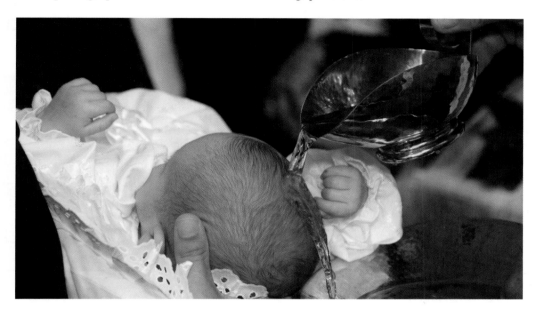

AQA
Examiner's tip
Remember that the photograph is there as a stimulus which you can make use of in your answer and which can often give you important hints.

(a)   Explain the meaning of **two** symbols used during the Roman Catholic rite of infant baptism.   *(4 marks)*

AQA
Examiner's tip
In (a) you are asked to explain the meaning of two symbols. You will not be given any credit if you just give a list of all the symbols used, nor will you gain marks for dealing with more than two symbols.

(b)   Explain **one** way in which infant baptism might help the believer.   *(3 marks)*

AQA
Examiner's tip
In (b), you are given 3 marks to explain one way in which infant baptism helps the believer. This means that you have to develop the answer fairly fully in relation to this one way, and you will not gain marks for mentioning other ways.

(c)   'Confirmation should not be given to anyone under the age of twenty.' What do you think? Explain your opinion.   *(3 marks)*

(d)   'Christians do not need rites of passage.' What do you think? Explain your opinion.   *(3 marks)*

AQA
Examiner's tip
The two evaluation questions here are only worth 3 marks each. You have to express your own view and explain why you hold that view. You do not have to examine any other views in these questions.

3.1 Buildings used for worship: external features

Worship and buildings

Worship is giving time and honour to God. Many Christians worship in private but they also appreciate the need to come together as a community to worship God. For this reason, most Christian denominations have specific places where the community can meet. These places are usually called either **churches** or chapels. Each Christian denomination may adapt their building for worship so that the main features reflect the importance of particular aspects of worship for that denomination.

Many Christians believe that the community of believers is more important than the place that the community meets. The church building is simply a meeting place for the Church. Some people take the view that the church building should be simple and functional. Others are of the opinion that a church is the house of God and so should be very impressive. They believe that nothing is too good for God and that this should be reflected in the church buildings.

Exterior features of Christian places of worship

Most Christian denominations tend to use features on the outside of their buildings to stress the fact that this is a place of worship. Many church buildings are taller than the surrounding buildings, though this is not so common in city centres. Many churches have towers or steeples. These features help the church to stand out from other buildings as something special that can be recognised as such, even by non-believers. Towers and steeples represent prayer and worship rising up to heaven, a physical representation of what takes place inside the building.

Objectives

Understand what churches are.

Appreciate how church buildings can be recognised from outside.

Evaluate the need for distinctive church buildings.

Key terms

Church: a building in which Christians worship.

∞ links

For more on worship see Chapter 4.

AQA Examiner's tip

You need to be able to comment on the different external features and how useful you think they are for Christians.

A Many churches have towers to stand out from the surrounding buildings

The approach of modern church building tends to be simpler than it was fifty years ago. Towers and steeples are less common but the church buildings still tend to stand out because of their external design. Many denominations do not believe in spending too much money on church buildings, preferring to spend their money on works of charity. They choose not to have features that seem to have little practical use, like towers and steeples. However, they like to show that their building is a place of worship, usually by having a very prominent cross outside. It is also usual practice to have large noticeboards outside every church to announce when the services and other meetings are. The aim of these is to make sure that everybody is informed about what is happening so that everybody feels welcome to come into the place of worship.

B   *Many modern churches stand out but do not have towers*

Research activity

1   Examine five different Christian churches in your neighbourhood. Draw up a chart to show which features (e.g. towers, prominent buildings) are most common among them.

Activities

1   Explain why many Christians want to have church buildings.

2   Explain two ways in which church buildings can be identified from the outside.

3   'Christian places of worship should not stand out from other buildings.' Do you agree? Give reasons for your answer, showing that you have thought about more than one point of view.

Research activity

2   Choose five different Christian denominations and explain how the external features of their churches or chapels reflect the denominations' understanding of the role of the place of worship.

Extension activity

Research how the external features of churches have changed over the last 300 years, especially comparing modern Roman Catholic churches with those built when it was not acceptable to be a Roman Catholic (in the 17th and 18th centuries).

Summary

You should now know what churches are and be able to explain how church buildings can be recognised from outside. You should also have some thoughts about the need for distinctive church buildings.

Buildings used for worship: a Roman Catholic church

The interior of a Roman Catholic church

The interior of Roman Catholic churches can vary from being very ornate to fairly plain. The whole church is focused on the **sanctuary**, literally the holy place. This is where the altar, the lectern and the tabernacle are. The sanctuary is where all the public worship is centred. Roman Catholic churches are also designed to allow people to use the building for private worship.

The following table describes the common features in Roman Catholic churches.

A

	Name of feature	What it is and how it helps worship
	The **altar**	A table-like structure, usually of a type of stone. This is the place where the bread and wine are offered to God and are changed into the Body and Blood of Christ. An altar is a place of sacrifice, where praise is given to God.
	The **lectern** or reading stand	The place where the Word of God is proclaimed when the readings from scripture take place.
	The **pulpit**	A raised structure from which the priest preaches. In many churches this structure will be used as the lectern as well as the pulpit.
	The **tabernacle**	A small cupboard-like structure which is used to keep the consecrated hosts (wafers) that can be taken for the Communion for the sick. The tabernacle can also be a focus for private worship. Many Roman Catholics like to pray quietly in front of the Blessed Sacrament (the name given to the consecrated bread and wine) because they believe that Christ is fully present in the consecrated host.
	The **sanctuary lamp**	A red lamp which is kept burning to show the Real Presence of Christ in the bread in the tabernacle. It is a reminder to people of the continual love of God and it shows strangers to the church where the Blessed Sacrament is kept reserved for private worship.
	The baptistery or baptismal font	Used to be by the main door to the church to show that people entered the Church through baptism. Now the font tends to be an item of church furniture which can be moved so that all those present can easily see a baptism when it takes place.
	Statues	Usually found around the church to help people to pray and to ask their favourite saint to intercede for them.
	The **Stations of the Cross**	Fourteen plaques or carvings on the walls, representing the different events during the journey Jesus took to his Crucifixion. They help people to pray.
	Stained glass windows	They brighten God's house and to make it a place worthy of praising God.
	The **Lady altar**	A side altar dedicated to Mary, the mother of Jesus. This is usually a place of quiet, private prayer and it encourages Catholics to offer devotion to Mary.

Case study

St George's Roman Catholic Church, Liverpool

St George's first church was built in 1887 when the parish was in a rural district. As the city spread out, there was a need for a bigger church. A larger, brick building was constructed in 1929 that could hold 250 people at any Mass. After the Second Vatican Council in 1965, when there were major changes in the way Mass was said, St George's church was modernised. The old altar against the back wall was removed and replaced with a simple marble table-like structure, set so that the priest could face the congregation. A lectern in marble was also built beside the altar to allow the readers to be clearly heard and seen so that the word of God could be understood. The organ was also brought down to the floor of the church so that all the members of the congregation could be encouraged to join in the singing. More space was needed, so two side wings were added at right angles to the altar. This means that nobody is very far from the altar.

Key terms

Stations of the Cross: a series of images or pictures in a church of the events of Jesus' trial and execution.

AQA Examiner's tip

Remember that the central features of a Roman Catholic church are the altar, the pulpit and the tabernacle.

Activities

1. Explain how the interior of a Roman Catholic church is structured so that the focus is on the celebration of the Mass and the Blessed Sacrament.

2. Explain how the interior of a Roman Catholic church is structured so that it helps people to worship both collectively and as individuals.

3. 'A Roman Catholic church does not need a lectern or pulpit.' Do you agree? Give reasons for your answer, showing that you have thought about more than one point of view.

Research activity

Visit a Roman Catholic church. Produce a document that shows how the common features described in Table **A** appear in that church.

Extension activity

Compare a Roman Catholic church built in the 19th century (one that has kept many of its original features) with a Roman Catholic church built within the last 25 years.

B *The interior of a Roman Catholic church*

Discussion activity

Should church buildings be changed to allow for more modern celebrations of the services or should they remain as they were originally designed? Discuss with a partner or in a small group, justifying your opinion.

Summary

You should now be able to explain the interior structure of a typical Roman Catholic church, with the focus on the altar, lectern and tabernacle, and how this structure helps believers to worship. You should also be able to evaluate the need for the main features in a Roman Catholic church.

Buildings used for worship: Roman Catholic and Anglican churches

A *Inside a Roman Catholic Church*

The Church of England is often called the Anglican Church. At the Reformation in the 16th century, Henry VIII and Elizabeth I broke away from the Roman Catholic Church and started an independent Church. The services were often based on preaching the word of God from the Bible. However, there has always been a Communion service as a major

B *Inside an Anglican church*

element in Anglican worship. This means that Anglican churches have kept the altar as a central feature. The pulpit, lectern and baptismal font are also important features that are found in Anglican churches. Because most Anglicans do not believe in Transubstantiation (see page 114), there is no tabernacle or sanctuary lamp in most Anglican churches.

There is a wide range of opinion and practice within the Anglican community about how much decoration there should be inside a church. Few Anglican churches have statues or the Stations of the Cross, but many churches do have stained glass windows. There tend to be fewer decorations of any kind in an Anglican church when compared to a Roman Catholic church.

C   *Few Anglican churches have statues or Stations of the cross but many churches have stained glass windows*

Activities

2   Compare the picture of the Anglican church (**B**) with the one of the Roman Catholic church (**A**). What are the similarities and the differences?

3   'The simpler style of Anglican churches is better to help people worship.' Do you agree? Give reasons for your answer, showing that you have thought about more than one point of view.

Summary

You should now be able to explain the differences between Roman Catholic and Anglican churches and appreciate how these differences in features reflect differences in the styles of worship.

Extension activity

1   Visit an Anglican church and a Roman Catholic church and make a list of all the differences you notice.

Research activities

1   Examine how the following items are used by the Anglican Church in their worship: the altar, the pulpit, the font, the organ, the choir.

2   Compare a modern Anglican church with an older Anglican church. What are the main similarities and differences that you notice?

Extension activity

2   Try to find a place of worship that is shared between different Christian denominations (there are small chapels in most hospitals and airports if there is not a shared church locally). What differences do you notice between this place of worship and a church used by just one denomination?

Orthodox churches are usually far more elaborate than buildings for worship in most other Christian denominations. There is a great use of colour, with richly decorated vestments (clothes worn by the priests) being worn during the service and very ornate decoration throughout the church.

External features

Most Orthodox churches look imposing from the outside. They tend to be rectangular buildings, representing the ark of salvation. The ark that saved Noah and his family from drowning is a symbol of the saving from sin that comes through Christ and the Church. The cupolas or domes of the church represent the heavens above. Many Orthodox churches have onion-shaped domes, topped with crosses, which make them very prominent buildings.

Internal features

The most prominent internal feature of an Orthodox church is the **iconostasis**. This is a screen covered in icons (religious images of Jesus, Mary, the angels and the saints) that goes across the whole width of the church. The screen represents the division between heaven and earth.

In front of the iconostasis is the nave. This is where the congregation of believers stand. Believers are usually separated into men on the right-hand side of the church and women on the left. This is to show the equality of men and women before God. However, it also continues the Jewish practice of men and women being separate in the synagogue. People stand for prayer in the Orthodox Church.

Behind the screen is the sanctuary, which contains the altar. The altar is called the royal throne or holy table. What is done at the altar is so holy that it is removed from the sight of normal people. Only the priests and deacons (ordained assistants to the priests) may enter the sanctuary. Behind the altar is the bishop's chair or throne.

In the middle of the iconostasis are the **Royal Doors**, behind which there is a curtain. The Royal Doors are closed for most of the service (which is called the Liturgy – see Chapter 5) except for three occasions:

- When the priest carries the book of the Gospels through the Royal Doors to show them to the people.
- When the priest receives the offerings of bread, wine and money and they are taken through the Royal Doors and placed on the altar.
- After the consecration, when the bread and wine are brought out and given to the people in Communion.

Each of these moments reflects heaven and earth coming closer together.

Objectives

Understand the internal and external structure of an Orthodox church.

Appreciate how the internal structure aids worship.

Evaluate the need for decoration in an Orthodox church.

links

You can find out more about icons on page 84, and you can see a photograph of the interior of an Orthodox church on page 117.

A St Basil's Orthodox Cathedral, Moscow

B *An iconostasis*

There are two smaller doors either side of the Royal Doors that are used for the deacons to enter the sanctuary.

In front of the Royal Doors there are often two large candle stands that represent the light that led the Jews through the wilderness into the Promised Land.

Above the main church there is a very heavily decorated domed ceiling which represents the heavens, where God is. The picture on the dome is of the Pantokrator, the Creator of the universe.

Research activity

Using the internet, find out as much information as you can, including photographs, about Orthodox churches.

Activities

1. Explain **two** features in the Orthodox church that relate to the way in which the Liturgy takes place.

2. 'Orthodox churches reflect the idea that there is nothing too good for God.' Do you agree? Give reasons for your answer, showing that you have thought about more than one point of view.

Summary

You should now be able to describe the internal and external structure of a typical Orthodox church, and explain how the focus on the iconostasis, the Royal Doors and the elaborate decoration helps believers to worship. You should also be able to express an opinion about the need for decoration in an Orthodox church.

AQA Examiner's tip

You are expected to know what features the churches have in common, and will also need to know about their distinctive features. It is worth having a selection of points that you can refer to about at least one place of worship.

Discussion activity

Should there be a lot of decorations in churches? Discuss with a partner or in a small group, justifying your opinion.

Extension activity

Make a portfolio of all the symbols and symbolic features that are used in an Orthodox church. Explain what each of the features is and why it is an important element in the church.

Buildings used for worship: the non-conformist traditions (1)

The non-conformist traditions

Non-conformists are those Christians who broke away from any control by a government and who do not conform to particular religious practices. They strongly believe in the importance of the word of God as found in the Bible and they reject the ordained ministries of priests and bishops, but some churches ordain their ministers. Non-conformist services are pulpit-centred, as the word of God is proclaimed from the pulpit. Most will hold Communion services, but the altar or table may be smaller than in a Roman Catholic church. Also, it is often movable because Communion is not such a central part of their worship.

Most modern non-conformist churches or chapels have very flexible seating arrangements. This is so that the minister can organise a particular service in the way he or she wants. There may be no statues or stained glass in their chapels and decorations of any type may be limited. Many non-conformists do not believe that anything should distract them from their worship of God. From the outside, most non-conformist chapels look fairly plain, with no towers or ornate stonework. However, the buildings always give the feel of a place of worship.

There are many non-conformist Churches, including the Baptists, the Methodists, the United Reformed Church and the Quakers (Society of Friends). All of these are independent of each other and yet they all share many common features. On these two pages and the next two, we shall look at the buildings used for worship by three of these Churches:

- **Quakers**, who form a Christian group that has no specific leader and that gathers to be inspired by the Holy Spirit.

- **Baptists** and **Methodists**, who are fairly typical of Christians who gather together in chapels, usually led by a minister, to offer worship. Their buildings are very similar to those of the United Reformed Church.

The Quaker tradition

A Quaker Meeting House will be very plain both inside and outside. In the main meeting room, there will be a group of chairs centred around a simple table on which is placed a Bible and possibly a vase of flowers. No other religious symbol is used. There is no baptistery or Communion table because Quakers do not have either baptism or Holy Communion.

Quakers come and sit in silence until someone feels inspired by the Holy Spirit to say something, to read from the Bible or to offer a prayer.

Objectives

Know how typical non-conformist chapels are structured.

Appreciate how this structure aids worship in these Churches.

Evaluate the need for simplicity in places of worship.

AQA *Examiner's tip*

You will not be asked about any specific non-conformist Church but you need to be aware of the arguments used to support different types of worship and buildings used for worship.

A *A minister preaching in a church typical of the non-conformist tradition*

B   *Inside Bull Street Quaker Meeting House, Birmingham*

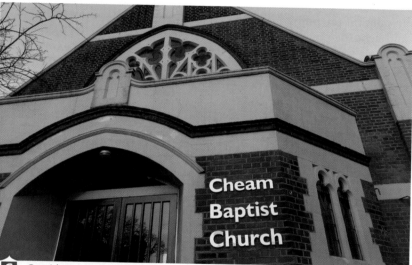

Cheam
Baptist
Church

C   *Outside a typical non-conformist place of worship*

Activities

1   State five ways in which a non-conformist chapel would be different from a Roman Catholic or Anglican church.

2   Explain how the features and structure of non-conformist chapels reflect the type of worship that takes place there.

3   'All churches should be pulpit-centred.' Do you agree? Give reasons for your answer, showing that you have thought about more than one point of view.

Research activity

Choose a non-conformist church in your area. Do a project to show how their place of worship is structured and how this reflects the type of worship that takes place there.

Activities

4   Explain how the structure of a Quaker Meeting House helps the Friends (members of the Society) to worship.

5   'It is essential that when Christians pray, there is nothing about that will distract them.' Do you agree? Give reasons for your answer, showing that you have thought about more than one point of view.

Summary

You should now be able to describe the structure of typical non-conformist places of worship, and explain how this structure helps believers to worship. You should also have some views about whether there is a need for simplicity in places of worship.

Buildings used for worship: the non-conformist traditions (2)

The Baptist tradition

Unlike the Roman Catholic tradition, in which there are fairly strict rules about what has to be included in a church building, the Baptist tradition is very flexible. However, from a practical point of view, some elements will always be included.

- In Baptist worship, the main act of worship is based on the Bible. For this reason, the focal point of the chapel is the pulpit.

- A typical Sunday service comprises: a hymn, a series of prayers of praise, Bible readings, prayers of intercession (when people ask God for things), a collection, a hymn, a sermon, a final hymn and a blessing.

- Near the pulpit there will be a table that will be used to celebrate Communion. This might be under the pulpit if the pulpit is raised high for all the congregation to see and hear the preacher, or to one side of the pulpit.

- The church will often be quite plain. There may be a single large cross visible in the chapel, but there will be few, if any, other decorations. Baptists do not believe in the use of statues or icons but might display banners to represent church organisations or Scout and Guide flags.

- In Baptist chapels there will be a baptistery at the front of the church. For safety's sake, if there is no baptism taking place at the time, the pool is often covered over and will not be seen.

- Most Baptist chapels have a flexible arrangement of chairs so that the minister can organise them to suit the occasion, depending on the kind of service planned.

Objectives

Know how typical Baptist and Methodist chapels are structured.

Appreciate how these structures aid worship in these Churches.

Evaluate the need for non-conformist places of worship.

Discussion activity

Should a lot of money be spent on Christian places of worship? Discuss with a partner or in a small group, justifying your opinion.

Research activity

1 Visit a local Baptist chapel and create a leaflet that shows the importance of the chapel as a place of worship and as a meeting place. Investigate all the activities that take place in that building. Why do Baptists use their chapels for activities other than worship?

A *The interior of a Baptist church*

Methodist churches

The Methodist Church tends to have a more formal structure in its services than the Baptist church. The Methodist worship is mainly Bible-based so the pulpit and reading stand (lectern) are the central features of most Methodist churches. Singing is an essential part of their services so there is a place for an organ or musicians in the building. Before the use of microphones, it was important that the congregation could hear the preacher. Because of this churches were built so that as many people as possible could be near the front. This meant that seating was often on balconies, overlooking the pulpit. Once or twice a month there is a Communion service so Methodist churches usually have a Communion table near the pulpit area. Many Methodist Churches practise infant baptism so there is often a baptismal bowl or font in a fairly prominent place.

B   *Inside a Methodist church*

Summary

You should now be able to explain how many Baptist and Methodist churches are structured, and understand how these structures aid worship in these churches. You should also have an opinion about whether special places of worship are needed for these traditions.

3.7 Pilgrimage: introduction

What is pilgrimage?

A **pilgrimage** is a journey to a holy place. It is an opportunity for believers to focus on their journey to God.

In the Middle Ages, when people travelled only on foot or on donkeys, it would take days, weeks or even years to make a pilgrimage. Because of this it was seen as something very special. Nowadays, with transport being quicker and more comfortable, it is easier to make a pilgrimage. The demands seem less great and for some people there is less to be obtained from going on a pilgrimage.

Many people still go on pilgrimages, whether for a day of prayer or as part of a holiday. In some ways, life is a pilgrimage, and physically going on a pilgrimage can help believers to ponder on their life's journey.

Why do Christians go on pilgrimage?

The main reasons people go on pilgrimage are:

- as an act of prayer and devotion
- to help strengthen their faith
- to share the experience and their faith with other believers
- to increase their sense of belonging to a wider Church community
- to be able to relate more closely to the events or the people associated with the place of pilgrimage
- to pray for something special
- as a way of thanking God for something they have received
- to do a penitential act (an action that causes some pain or discomfort) as a reflection of sorrow for sin
- to come closer to God by giving him time and attention
- to care for the sick and handicapped who want to go on a pilgrimage but cannot do so on their own
- to strengthen their belief that God has a special place in their lives
- to seek healing, whether it is physical, spiritual or emotional.

Objectives

Examine what pilgrimage is and why Christians go on pilgrimage.

Examine the different types of places of pilgrimage.

Evaluate the need for pilgrimage.

Key terms

Pilgrimage: a journey by a Christian to a holy site, e.g. Lourdes.

Activities

1 Explain what a pilgrimage is.

2 Look at the list of reasons that people go on pilgrimage. Which reasons do you think are the best and which the worst for going on pilgrimage? Explain your answer.

3 'People go on pilgrimage only to get a healing miracle.' Do you agree? Give reasons for your answer, showing that you have thought about more than one point of view.

A Disabled pilgrims being cared for

■ Types of pilgrimage

The sites that people choose to visit on pilgrimages can be roughly divided into three categories:

1 **Famous international sites**, such as the Holy Land, Rome and Lourdes. These pilgrimages usually last for more than four days and, because of the numbers of pilgrims, these sites can be very focused on religious activities.

2 **Shrines connected with notable saints and apparitions**, such as Assisi (St Francis), Lisieux (St Thérèse), Compostela (St James), Knock in Ireland (Mary, St Joseph, St John and Jesus) and Walsingham in Norfolk (Mary). Visits here are often part of a journey and the visit to the shrine might only take two or three days.

B St Thérèse's Basilica, Lisieux

3 **Local shrines**, such as St Winifride's Well (Holywell), Lindisfarne (especially Holy Island), the grave of Blessed Dominic Barberi (St Helens) and Mount Grace (Osmotherly, North Yorks) that can be visited for a few hours and tend to attract only Christians from neighbouring parishes.

Summary

You should now be able to explain what a pilgrimage is, the main reasons that Christians go on pilgrimage, and the different types of pilgrimage sites. You should also be able to evaluate the importance of pilgrimage.

AQA Examiner's tip

You will not be asked about any specific pilgrimage site on the exam paper, but you will be expected to give detailed references to one site that you have studied. Choose one that you are interested in or that you can obtain a lot of information about.

Discussion activity

Is it right to think of pilgrimage as a symbol of the journey of life? Discuss with a partner or in a small group, justifying your opinion.

Activity

4 Draw up a leaflet encouraging Christians to visit a shrine that is local to you. (There is almost certainly one within 50 miles of your home.)

Research activity

Using the internet, find out as much as you can about two different places of pilgrimage from groups 1 and 2 above.

Extension activity

Choose one place of pilgrimage. Do a research project on this place including:

■ the importance of the saint or event connected with this place

■ its history

■ the things that pilgrims do there

■ the meaningfulness of this place for the pilgrims.

3.8 Places of pilgrimage: the Holy Land

The Holy Land

The Holy Land (Israel and Palestine) is the place where Jesus was born and raised, where he taught and where he died. Consequently there are a great many sites connected with the events of his life and death in the Holy Land. As a result a pilgrimage to these sites is a high spot of many believers' lives. The places of pilgrimage include the following:

- **Bethlehem**, especially the **Church of the Nativity**, which marks the site where Jesus was born and laid in a manger. Pilgrims like to see the place where God revealed his love for humanity by becoming man.
- The **Sea of Galilee**, scene of Jesus' major teachings. To follow in the footsteps that Jesus took means that Christians can see themselves as real followers, 'disciples'.
- **Jerusalem**, which contains many Christian shrines, especially:
  - **Gethsemane**, the garden in which Jesus passed his last night and where he was arrested. Christians can join here in prayer remembering the prayer that Jesus offered before his arrest.
  - The **Church of the Holy Sepulchre**, which is believed to be built over both Golgotha, where Jesus died, and the tomb from which he rose. Christians can focus on the central events in the Christian faith and in their salvation.
  - The **Via Dolorosa** (the Way of Sorrow). According to tradition, this is the route taken by Jesus from Pilate's palace to Golgotha, the place of the Crucifixion. Many pilgrims walk the route barefoot. This allows them to join in with the sufferings of Jesus, which he underwent out of love for humanity.

By sharing in the life story, ministry and death of Jesus, Christians believe that they can become closer to Jesus and appreciate the beginnings of the Christian faith more fully.

A The doorway to the Church of the Nativity

B The Garden of Gethsemane

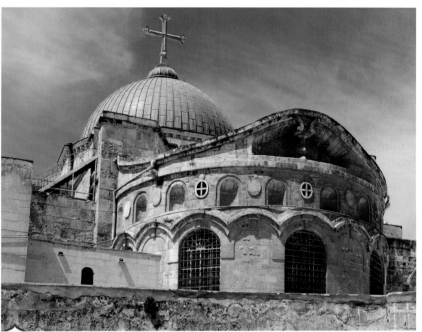

C *The Church of the Holy Sepulchre*

Research activity

Investigate on the internet what religious activities Christians can do in the Holy Land, explaining how these activities might help a Christian's faith.

Activities

1   Why do many Christians like to visit the Holy Land?

2   'Every Christian should go on pilgrimage to the Holy Land.' Do you agree? Give reasons for your answer, showing that you have thought about more than one point of view.

A pilgrim's experience in the Holy Land

'It was while we were visiting the Church of the Nativity in Bethlehem that an incident occurred which became for all of us the highlight of the holiday. We entered a rectangular-shaped cave lit by forty-eight lamps and we felt we were standing in the very birthplace of Christ. A silver star with the Latin inscription *"Hic de Maria Virgine Jesus Christus natus est"* (Here Christ was born of the Virgin Mary) marks the spot. A little to the right down a couple of steps lay the Holy Manger. The primitive rock, blackened by the smoke of candles and lamps, may be seen above the manger.

Whilst our guide was telling us the history of the church, a most moving, yet simple, event happened. Completely oblivious to our group a young mother came into the cave with a baby in her arms and a small child held by the hand. After kneeling in prayer she gently laid the baby onto the centre of the star for a few moments as an act of faith, picked up the baby again and then quietly left. I am sure we were all affected by this act, so simple but beautiful.'

'Some of the Pilgrims', The Spire Magazine, December 1990

Case study

Activity

3   Why do you think the event related in this case study made an impact on the pilgrims?

Summary

You should now be able to explain why the Holy Land is an important area for pilgrimage for most Christians, and evaluate the usefulness of such pilgrimages.

Shrines to Mary

Many places of pilgrimage are dedicated to **Mary**, whom Catholics often call 'Our Lady'. Some of these, such as Walsingham in Norfolk, go back to the Middle Ages whereas others are very recent. The most popular of these shrines in Europe are Lourdes (in France) and Fatima (in Portugal). Most shrines are in places where people have claimed to see visions of Mary.

Lourdes

Lourdes is in south-west France. In 1858 a young girl, Bernadette Soubirous, had a number of visions of Our Lady. The 'lady' called herself 'The Immaculate Conception', a title that had been recently defined as an official teaching of the Roman Catholic Church.

The lady told Bernadette to dig for a spring. This spring has healing qualities and many people bathe in the water on their pilgrimage.

The lady also asked for a church to be built and for people to come there in procession. Now every day there are thousands of pilgrims, including those who are very sick, who come to pray at the grotto (the rock opening where Mary appeared) and recite the rosary together.

Pilgrim activities

- Each evening there is a candlelight procession (this is always referred to as the torchlight procession). There is also a procession of the Blessed Sacrament (the consecrated bread that Roman Catholics believe is the Body and Blood of Christ).

- Many people also go up in the hills and take part in the Stations of the Cross, as a form of penance and prayer.

- Many Catholics who cannot get to Lourdes often ask pilgrims to light a candle at the grotto for them.

- Most pilgrims attend Mass either in the basilica (large church) or in one of the neighbouring churches.

- Many pilgrims, especially the sick, bathe in the water from the spring.

- Regular services are held for the sick, especially the anointing of the sick.

- Priests are always available to hear confessions.

- Many pilgrims also visit the home of Bernadette and her family to help them feel closer to a central character of Lourdes' history.

Objectives

Examine pilgrimage to shrines connected with Mary.

Appreciate how visiting these shrines might help Roman Catholics in their faith.

Evaluate the need to go to distant shrines.

Key terms

Mary: the mother of Jesus. Mary is held in great honour by many Christians as the Mother of God.

∞links

You can find out about the rosary on page 85.

A *Candlelight procession at Lourdes*

Walsingham

Walsingham, in Norfolk, was a very popular shrine in the Middle Ages, connected with a vision of Mary. A replica of the Holy Family's house at Nazareth was contained within the Priory grounds. The house and shrine were destroyed on the orders of Henry VIII.

It is the national Roman Catholic shrine in England today.

Pilgrim activities

- People process from the old Priory grounds to the Slipper Chapel, often carrying a statue of Our Lady of Walsingham.
- Some people walk the last mile, the Holy Mile, barefoot, following the tradition of the Middle Ages.
- People recite the rosary together.
- Pilgrims go to Mass and often go to confession, to get rid of their sins.
- The sick and the handicapped are well looked after, following the same type of activities as at Lourdes (but there is no spring to bathe in).

B *Outside the Church of the Annunciation at Walsingham*

Activity

'There is no need to go abroad to go on a pilgrimage.' Do you agree? Give reasons for your answer, showing that you have thought about more than one point of view.

Research activity 🔍

Choose one shrine other than Lourdes or Walsingham that is connected to Mary and research what happens at that shrine. Other shrines might include: Loretto, Guadalupe, Czestochowa, Knock, Fatima.

Summary

You should now know about pilgrimage to shrines connected with Mary and appreciate how visiting these shrines might help Roman Catholics in their faith. You should also have some thoughts about the usefulness of visiting shrines in distant places.

Extension activity

Draw up a chart of places associated with Mary, showing their historical importance and their popularity.

Case study

Student Cross celebrates 60 years of pilgrimage

The oldest annual pilgrimage in Britain celebrated its diamond anniversary in 2008 when more than 250 pilgrims walked around 120 miles during Holy Week.

Student Cross, which began in 1948, started on Friday 14 March and finished in Walsingham, Norfolk, on Easter Sunday.

David Ring, National Organiser of Student Cross for 2008, said: 'Student Cross is a week which is physically demanding but spiritually uplifting. Being on pilgrimage together helps us grow in all sorts of unexpected ways.

'We lead (and occasionally drag) each other out of our comfort zones – physical, social, spiritual – through some tough walking, refreshing liturgy, and close friendship. It is a very tiring journey but spirits are constantly raised by the people we walk with and by the parishioners we meet and who help us on our routes.'

The pilgrimage is made up of ten groups or 'Legs' who walk to Walsingham to meet and celebrate the Easter weekend. Each leg carries a large wooden cross as a visible witness to their Christian faith.

www.studentcross.org.uk

Objectives

Examine how people claim to feel after a pilgrimage.

See the relevance of pilgrimage in the believer's life.

Evaluate the need for pilgrimage.

How people feel after a pilgrimage

Many people go on a pilgrimage because of some type of pressure. It could be from a sense of needing to do something about major problem areas in their life. It might be to help a disabled person have a holiday, often stimulated by a mixture of charity and an awareness, perhaps, of a little guilt. This may come from feeling that they are the lucky ones who don't need looking after so they ought to help those who do. Sometimes people feel restless about a part of their life that they want to do something about, even though often they do not know exactly what the restlessness is caused by. Some people feel that they have lost a sense of God in their life and want to find him again. Others go just to be with friends on a different type of holiday.

Whatever the motives for going on pilgrimage, the way people feel after the event may not have much to do with their initial motive. A pilgrimage is a group event. It helps an individual to feel part of the Church community in a major way. Pilgrims work together, pray together and, most importantly, feel accepted by each other. This makes the individuals realise that God accepts them and is concerned about their lives.

The tensions that people feel before the pilgrimage often vanish during the journey, which is often a journey of self-discovery. This does not mean that the problems people faced disappear but it does mean that people feel more able to deal with the problems. This is most noticeably true with those who are sick. Very few people come back from pilgrimage with their illness cured or even eased. However, they

A *Priests and bishops often join lay Christians on their pilgrimage to give spiritual support*

do come back feeling at peace in themselves and able to accept and cope with the problems that face them. By discovering themselves and being at peace, many people learn how to value the role of God in their life in a new way.

Discussion activity

'Do pilgrimages change anything?' Discuss this question with a partner or in a small group, justifying your opinion.

B   *People visiting chapels at Lourdes*

Research activities

1   Interview a person who has been on a pilgrimage and ask them to explain how their life has been affected by this experience.

2   Look on the internet for an account of a pilgrimage. Write a summary of the importance of the pilgrimage for the pilgrims.

Activities

1   Many people feel happier after going to a shrine. In what ways might these people have benefited from their pilgrimage?

2   'All Christians should go on a pilgrimage at least once in their life.' Do you agree? Give reasons for your answer, showing that you have thought about more than one point of view.

Extension activity

Investigate a group that organises pilgrimages for others (e.g. the HCPT – The Pilgrimage Trust). What reasons for going on pilgrimage does the organisation offer?

Summary

You should now understand how people claim to feel after a pilgrimage, and appreciate the relevance of pilgrimage in a believer's life. You should also be able to express an opinion about the need to go on pilgrimage.

3

Places of worship – summary

For the examination you should now be able to:

✔ know and understand how the structure of Christian places of worship affects the worship taking place

✔ understand how the main exterior and interior features of Christian places of worship relate to beliefs and practices

✔ understand why people go on pilgrimage

✔ describe one place of Christian pilgrimage and the activities which take place there

✔ know what people do at a place of pilgrimage and how going on pilgrimage can affect a Christian or change an individual's life

✔ assess the value of places of worship and of pilgrimage for the believer.

Sample answer

1 Write an answer to the following exam question:

'Pilgrimages are just an excuse for a holiday.'

Do you agree? Give reasons for your answer, showing that you have thought about more than one point of view.

(6 marks)

2 Read the following sample answer.

Christians go on pilgrimage to offer part of their life to God. They could go to any place just to enjoy themselves but they have chosen to specifically go to a religious site. This means that the believer is putting God into an important part of their life, showing that God means more to them than just having a bit of fun. The effects of a pilgrimage will last much longer than the relaxation gained from sitting on a beach, so the pilgrimage cannot just be dismissed as a holiday. However, what is wrong with having a pilgrimage as part or even the whole of a holiday? God

is an important part of a believer's whole life, not just on Sundays, and combining a pilgrimage with a holiday is a good way of showing this. Many people cannot afford to both go on pilgrimage and pay for a holiday, so why not combine the delights of the two experiences. It must also be remembered that 'holiday' comes from 'holy day', the original time off work was so that time can be given to God among other things. I believe that there is nothing wrong with having a pilgrimage as a holiday. It is not just 'an excuse' for one.

3 With a partner, discuss the sample answer. Do you think there are other things that the student could have included in the answer?

4 What mark would you give this answer out of 6? (Look at the mark scheme in the Introduction on page 7 (AO2) before you attempt this.) What are the reasons for the mark you have given?

AQA Examination-style questions

1 Look at the photograph below and answer the following questions.

(a) Explain how the place of worship of **one** Christian denomination is designed to help the members of that denomination to worship God.

(6 marks)

(b) 'It is a waste of money to build places just for worship.' Do you agree? Give reasons for your answer, showing that you have thought about more than one point of view.

(6 marks)

(c) Explain what believers do at **one** place of Christian pilgrimage.

(6 marks)

 AQA Examiner's tip Remember when answering (c) that you only have to comment on one place of pilgrimage. If you only answer in general terms, without indicating the place of pilgrimage, you will only receive Level 2 marks.

(d) 'Christians should only go on pilgrimage to a local shrine.' Do you agree? Give reasons for your answer, showing that you have thought about more than one point of view.

(6 marks)

4 Worship

4.1 Worship and prayer

■ The meaning of worship

The idea behind **worship** is 'honour' or 'worth'. To honour someone is to treat them with great respect, recognising their value. Worth is the value we recognise in a person. We only worship something that is greater than us. By giving time to worship, we accept not only that the person we honour in this way has value but also that we and our worship are important to them.

Christians believe that only God is of true or ultimate worth and that only God should be worshipped. Worshipping anything else would be idolatry. There are many qualities that Christians also value, such as love, truth and justice. However, believers would argue that all of these flow from God and find their true meaning in God, and therefore their value is linked to the ultimate value that is God.

False gods?

Sam is a 30-year-old Christian man.

'I think that too many people have distorted values. Only God is really worthy of worship. Those people who fill their houses with pictures of football teams or film stars are worshipping false gods. These so-called stars are not bothered about other people. They are only bothered about how much money they can make from people who are stupid enough to be taken in. Of course, people do need to enjoy their free time. A football match and a film are good entertainment, well worth the time and money spent on the enjoyment. It is people who treat players like God who do not know what real worship is all about.'

Activities

1. Is there a difference between supporting and worshipping a football team? Suggest some actions that might indicate that a person worshipped a football player/team or a pop/film star. Do you think Christians would think this was idolatry?

2. What are Christians stating about God when they worship only God?

Worship can be shown in many ways. Offering praise to God, or doing what God wants out of obedience and love to him, are simple ways in which most believers show their commitment and worship.

Prayer is one major form of worship. It is directly speaking to God. Many Christians believe that prayer helps them to open up their minds to God. They sometimes talk about it as a conversation. In a

Objectives

Understand what is meant by worship.

Appreciate how worship and prayer are carried out.

Evaluate the importance of worship and prayer.

Key terms

Worship: showing respect and value for God.

Prayer: words of praise, thanks or sorrow, etc. offered to God.

Discussion activity

With a partner or in a small group, discuss the views expressed by Sam. Do you agree with them? Give reasons for your opinion.

AQA *Examiner's tip*

You need to be aware of how prayer is a form of both private and public worship.

conversation you have to listen to what the other person is saying as well as talk yourself. A lot of people think that prayer is only about saying specific words at the right time. However, many believers are happy just to be in the presence of God. For some believers, the best form of private prayer is being silent in God's presence. This is sometimes known as meditation.

∞links

You can find out more about meditation on page 82.

Case study

The old man and the priest

A priest often went into a Roman Catholic church about 4.00 p.m. and would see an old man in scruffy clothes sitting at the back of the church, looking at the tabernacle. On one occasion, the priest went up to the man and asked what he was doing. The man replied, 'I just like to come in and sit here. I look at him and he looks at me.' Months later, the priest went to visit the local hospital and the nurse asked him to have a word with an old man who never had any visitors. The priest found the old man from the church there. The priest said to the man that he understood he never had any visitors. The old man was a little surprised at this and he said, 'Every day at 4.00 p.m. he comes in and he sits there. And he looks at me and I look at him.'

Activities

3   What is prayer?

4   Why do many people like to pray?

5   What does this case study suggest to you about prayer?

Research activity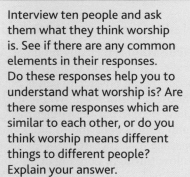

Interview ten people and ask them what they think worship is. See if there are any common elements in their responses. Do these responses help you to understand what worship is? Are there some responses which are similar to each other, or do you think worship means different things to different people? Explain your answer.

A   *Private prayer in church*

Extension activity

Interview a wide range of people (30 would be ideal) and ask them in what ways they prefer to offer worship. Ask them if they prefer to pray alone, with other people, using set prayers, spontaneously, aloud, in silence – and make a note of any other answer they give. Draw up a chart that reflects the different types of worship that are mentioned. If possible, draw a pie chart or graph that reflects the results you have gathered.

Summary

You should now be able to explain what the purpose of worship is and how prayer is a form of worship. You should also have some thoughts about the value of worship for the individual.

4.2 Private worship

Approaches to worship

There are two general approaches to worship:

- As an individual developing a one-to-one relationship with God; this is called private prayer or **private worship.**
- As part of a praying community, emphasising that each individual Christian is always a part of the Body of Christ, the Church community; this is normally called public worship.

Private worship

Many Christians give their own private time to God, worshipping him on their own as well as (or for some people instead of) gathering together with other people to worship God.

Prayer is personally communicating with God. Many people pray to God in the silence of their own room where there are no distractions. This means that they can focus on God alone, in whatever way seems appropriate at that time and for as long as the person desires.

It can be done spontaneously. This means that the individual just decides to pray to God simply because they want to do so. It also means that the way the prayer is phrased does not necessarily follow a structure.

Meditation: an approach to private prayer

Meditation is focusing on a particular object or thought to stimulate a prayer pattern and to help the person to concentrate when distractions occur. Being physically still is important when meditating. Many people choose a position that will help them to be comfortable for a long time. Many people put on a quiet piece of background music to create a calm atmosphere and to block out other distractions. Reading a short passage, possibly from the Bible, gives the person an idea that they can follow through. Looking at an object like a candle or a picture can help them to focus during the time of prayer.

A *Looking at objects such as candles or images of the sun rising can help worshippers to focus on prayer*

Objectives

Understand what private worship is and why it is important for believers.

Appreciate how meditation helps Christians to pray.

Evaluate the importance of private worship for the believer.

Key terms

Private worship: a believer giving God praise and worship on his or her own.

Meditation: being silent and thoughtful in the presence of God.

∞ links

You can find out more about spontaneous worship on page 87.

Activities

1. Why do some people prefer to be on their own when they pray?

2. 'The freedom to pray when you want is the best part of private worship.' Do you agree? Explain your opinion.

AQA Examiner's tip

You need to be aware of the nature and purpose of prayer in general and meditation as a specific form of prayer.

Activity

3. Try to meditate. It will take time and effort to make it meaningful but it can be a very positive experience. You do not have to believe in God to meditate.

B *At prayer*

Meditation produces an area of quiet in a busy life. This enables the person praying to get to the deeper aspects of life, to get down to the root of their being and to find God there. The sense of being in the presence of God and feeling at home there can strengthen the relationship with God. In the same way it is possible to sit next to a close friend and not feel the need to speak – you just share the moment together, building up the relationship in this way.

The importance of private prayer for the believer

Private prayer helps the individual believer to get closer to God in a very personal way. It helps them to follow Jesus' commands in the Sermon on the Mount:

> ### Beliefs and teachings
>
> But when you pray, go into your room, close the door and pray to your Father, who is unseen. Then your Father, who sees what is done in secret, will reward you.
>
> *Matthew* 6:6

Private prayer can be done whenever a person wants to make contact with God. It does not have to be at a set time. However, some people like to ensure they give time to prayer by always doing it at the same time every day. Prayer can make believers aware that God is in control of their life so they have nothing to be afraid of, even when times are hard. Some people compare their lives to the open seas: on the surface there are high waves and a lot of difficulties, but just below the surface things are calm. Believers think that since they can trust God, they can handle life's problems in a positive way. Prayer is one way that they can stay close to God and this enables them to keep a certain balance in their lives.

Activity

4 'Prayer keeps a person sane.' Do you agree? Give reasons for your answer, showing that you have thought about more than one point of view.

Discussion activity

With a partner or in a small group, discuss the following statement: 'It is impossible to empty your mind just to focus on God.' Give reasons for your opinion.

Research activity

Do a short survey about the ways in which people prefer to pray privately. Many people might initially say that they do not pray. Ask them what they do when something terrible happens, e.g. do they ask God for help, repeat a prayer they might have picked up at school or do they just rely on themselves to get through the problem?

Summary

You should now be able to explain what the purpose of private worship is and how meditation is used in private worship. You should also have some thoughts about the importance of private prayer.

Many Christians like to use **aids to worship**. These help them to maintain concentration when praying or worshipping. Some people find that they prefer to use one particular aid and that this helps them greatly when concentrating on their prayers.

Statues

Some people use **statues** to help them pray. A statue is a three-dimensional figure that represents Jesus, Mary or one of the saints.

Catholics do not pray to statues. They use the statue as a reminder of the person and the love of God that is reflected in that person. The statue is an aid to worship or to prayer. By looking at the statue, Catholics are able to concentrate on their prayers. They may ask the saint to pray with them and for them, in the belief that the saint is in the presence of God in heaven and can strengthen their prayers to God.

Some Catholics light a candle before a statue as an expression of offering prayers up to God through the intercession of the saint. Intercession is when you ask another person to add your prayers to theirs and to plead your cause for you.

Icons

An **icon** is a holy picture, specially painted to represent Christ, Mary or one of the saints. Icons are painted with special types of paint and use a lot of symbols. There is no attempt to make the painting lifelike but they help the believer to link to the person represented.

Icons are very important for Orthodox Christians. They see the icon as being filled with the spirit of the person whose image is shown on it. Some Christians believe that when you pray before an icon you come into direct contact with the person whose image is on the icon. Often Orthodox Christians burn candles or oil lamps in front of icons.

In all Orthodox churches there is an iconostasis. This is a screen containing a group of icons that separates the altar part of the church (the sanctuary) from the main body of the church where the people pray (the nave). This division represents the division between heaven and earth: the spiritual and the worldly. The iconostasis shows that the saints are now on the heavenly side of creation.

A An icon

The rosary

The **rosary** is a series of beads used by Roman Catholics during their prayers. Each bead represents a prayer and they are laid out in a series of one 'Our Father', ten 'Hail, Marys' and one 'Glory Be'.

- The **Our Father** is the name more commonly used by Roman Catholics for the Lord's Prayer.
- The **Hail, Mary** is a prayer addressed to Mary.
- The **Glory Be** is a prayer of praise addressed to the Trinity and it is often used at the end of a prayer to bring the prayer to a close.

Through using the rosary, Catholics hope to be able to focus on prayer. The repetitive nature of the prayer helps many Christians to keep a focus on what they are praying about. The fact that people do not need to think about what words they have to say means that they can think more deeply about the meaning of the prayer. Many Roman Catholics use the rosary as the starting point for meditation.

There are 20 **decades** of the rosary. A decade is the Our Father, ten Hail, Marys and the Glory Be that are said together. The decades are split into four groups and each one commemorates an important event in the life of Jesus and Mary. The rosary therefore helps Roman Catholics to reach into the heart of these important events.

 A rosary

Key terms

Rosary: a method of prayer, mainly used by Roman Catholics; the beads used during the praying of the Rosary.

Extension activity

Find out how icons are made and how valuable Orthodox Christians find them for prayer.

Beliefs and teachings

The Glory Be

The Glory Be to the Father and to the Son and to the Holy Spirit, as it was in the beginning, is now and ever shall be, world without end. Amen.

∞ links

For more on the Our Father see pages 94–95 and for more on the Hail, Mary see page 98.

Activities

3 Explain how Roman Catholics use the rosary when they pray.

4 'Aids to worship stop a believer coming close to God.' Do you agree? Give reasons for your answer, showing that you have thought about more than one point of view.

Research activity 🔍

2 Research three other items that people may use when they pray, e.g. the Bible, candles, incense, the Stations of the Cross. What are the items you have researched? How are they used? How do they help Christians in their prayer life?

Summary

You should now be able to explain how and why Christians make use of various aids to worship when they pray. You should also be able to evaluate the usefulness of aids to worship.

4.4 Forms of public worship

Public worship

In **public worship** Christians come together to worship God to show that they are the Body of Christ and need each other. Many Christians believe that without the support from other Christians both in practice and in example, their own individual routines of prayer, their prayer life, would become more difficult.

The Roman Catholic Church insists that Roman Catholics should attend Mass each Sunday as an offering of themselves to God. This is to remind themselves of their need for the support of others and in turn to be there to support others in their need.

Activities

1 Why do Christians gather together to worship?

2 'A Christian can pray best at home not in church.' Do you agree? Give reasons for your answer, showing that you have thought about more than one point of view.

Liturgical and non-liturgical worship

Different Christian denominations have different forms of worship but they can be divided into two basic types: **liturgical worship** and **non-liturgical worship**.

Liturgical worship

Liturgical worship follows a fixed pattern, a set order which can often be found in a prayer book or a missal. For example, every Mass has a clear structure that the priest follows, though there is some room for introducing variations. The structure and familiarity of the **liturgy** or service helps many people to feel at home in the service, even when it is at a church they do not normally attend.

A *The service this priest is conducting is liturgical*

Liturgical worship tends to remain unchanged down the years so there is a real sense of tradition. 'We are doing what the earlier Christians did. It has stood the test of time so it must have value.' It is usually full of symbolism and the worshippers usually understand the symbols.

Activities

3 Give two arguments in favour of liturgical worship and two arguments against it.

4 'Liturgical worship never changes and is boring.' Do you agree? Give reasons for your answer, showing that you have thought about more than one point of view.

Objectives

Know what forms of worship Christians use together.

Understand how the different forms of worship help believers.

Evaluate the usefulness of different forms of worship.

⚭ links

See Chapter 5 for information on the Mass, the celebration of the Eucharist.

Key terms

Public worship: Christians gathering together to praise God.

Liturgical worship: a church service which follows a set text or ritual.

Non-liturgical worship: a service which does not follow a set text or ritual.

Structured worship: worship which follows a fixed pattern, e.g. Mass has a clear set structure that the priest follows.

Research activity

1 Find five different types of liturgical worship, e.g. the Mass, Benediction. For each type, explain what makes it liturgical.

Non-liturgical worship

This includes both non-**structured** and **spontaneous worship**.

Non-structured worship

Non-liturgical worship does not have a set order of service that is written down in a prayer book. There is usually a mixture of hymns, prayers, readings, etc., which may be in the same order from week to week. Sometimes the minister or leader may decide the prayers and the theme of the service. This will give a particular service a structure but this will be different from what happens in other churches of that denomination.

These services tend to be Bible-based. There is less ritual or ceremony, and usually the ministers have a less prominent role than in liturgical services. Sometimes, as in the Quaker tradition, there is no leader and the people taking part wait for inspiration from the Holy Spirit.

The United Reformed and Baptist Churches are Churches with non-liturgical worship.

Spontaneous worship

Non-liturgical services may be more informal and, in some denominations, people may join in by speaking or shouting out as they feel inspired. Spontaneous worship is done on the spur of the moment when people feel the desire to praise God. It is possible for people to worship spontaneously wherever they are so it can be done both publicly and privately.

Charismatic worship happens in meetings when people allow the Holy Spirit to work through them using gifts (charisms) like speaking in tongues and prophecy. This is typical of worship in Pentecostal churches, where spontaneous worship is important. People who use this type of worship follow the advice of Paul, who says in the Bible:

B   *Spontaneous worship*

AQA   Examiner's tip

Make sure you know what type of worship is meant by liturgical, non-liturgical, spontaneous and structured. Do not get these terms the wrong way round.

> **Beliefs and teachings**
>
> In the same way, the Spirit helps us in our weakness. We do not know what we ought to pray for, but the Spirit himself intercedes for us with groans that words cannot express. And he who searches our hearts knows the mind of the Spirit, because the Spirit intercedes for the saints in accordance with God's will.
>
> *Romans* 8:26–27

Research activity

2   Interview either a minister or a member of a Church that uses non-liturgical worship. Ask them about how the services are structured. Do they think it important that each service is different? Does the structure help the whole congregation and individuals within the congregation to be relaxed and focused during the services?

Activities

5   Explain what is meant by spontaneous worship.

6   Give two arguments in favour of non-liturgical worship and two arguments against it.

7   'Spontaneous worship is frightening.' Do you agree? Give reasons for your answer, showing that you have thought about more than one point of view.

Summary

You should now be able to explain why some Christians prefer a liturgical (structured) form of worship and others prefer a non-liturgical form of worship, either non-structured or spontaneous. You should also be able to express your own opinion on the issue.

Extension activity

Investigate the charismatic movement and its forms of worship.

The impact of public worship on Roman Catholics

The Roman Catholic Church's teaching on public worship

The Roman Catholic Church teaches that every Catholic should attend Mass every Sunday (the Sabbath day). They must also receive Holy Communion and attend the sacrament of reconciliation at least once a year. These teachings help believers to keep the Commandment 'Keep the Sabbath day holy'.

By going to Mass (see Chapter 5), Catholics are taking part in the one great sacrifice of praise, the sacrifice of Jesus on the cross that led to his Resurrection.

The Mass is community worship; it cannot be celebrated alone.

Activities

1 Why does the Roman Catholic Church lay down guidelines for attending Mass and receiving Holy Communion?

2 'There is no need to attend Mass regularly.' Do you agree? Give reasons for your answer, showing that you have thought about more than one point of view.

The impact of public worship

Public worship stresses the fact that Roman Catholics are all united in the Body of Christ. It is impossible to be a Christian alone.

Community worship is an expression of the individual's desire to pray as a part of a whole community. It is recognising that no one is ever really alone when they pray. A simple example of this is that, because of the time differences around the world, a priest somewhere will be saying Mass every minute. As the Mass is the highest form of prayer, every time a Christian prays, those prayers are, in a real way, joining the great stream of praise that is being offered up to God. An individual also needs communal prayer to keep their own prayer life alive. This may be best seen through the true story told in the case study below.

Objectives

Know the importance given to public worship by the Roman Catholic Church.

Understand how public worship can affect a believer's lifestyle and attitudes.

Evaluate the need for public worship.

⚭links

Look back to pages 34–35 for information on the sacrament of reconciliation.

Research activity 🔍

1 Question Christians who regularly attend church. Ask them about how important the relationship between sharing the Mass and other forms of worship together and being involved in other parish activities are to them.

Case study

The burning coals

One day a parish priest was visiting his parishioners. He called at the door of a man whose name was on his list but whom the priest had never seen in church. The man invited the priest in and they sat down either side of an open coal fire. The man said to the priest, 'Yes, father, I am a Catholic but I do not believe I need to go to church to pray and to believe.' The priest did not say anything but after a minute he picked up the coal tongs. He took a burning piece of coal out of the fire and placed it on its own in the hearth. Very slowly, the coal lost its red heat and gradually went cold. The priest left the house.

Activity

3 What point was the priest making? Do you think his point is valid? Explain your answer.

During each person's life there are times when praying gets difficult. Sometimes the simple routine of attending a service is the only way to keep going at prayer. A good example of this is St Teresa of Avila, a 16th century nun. She said that she found prayer, especially the public reciting of the Office that she had to do as a nun, pointless and boring. She went through what she called 'the dark night of the soul'. This continued for fifteen years but eventually she became one of the greatest exponents on mystical prayer, the deepest form of prayer that people experience. Regular routines are seen as important for many Christians.

A   *St Teresa of Avila*

Seeing other people pray and asking them to pray for something that is important for someone else can also be inspiring. Some of the greatest pray-ers are older people. Their acceptance of life and contentment may often be the result of their lifelong search for God. This is a search that is centred on prayer, especially public prayer. They have something that most people want to share in and they can inspire others simply by being themselves.

Extension activity

1   Research two different forms of public worship other than the Mass that are used by Roman Catholics. Examples could be the public saying of the Prayer of the Church and Benediction.

Extension activity

2   Research the life of St Teresa of Avila.

Activity

4   'There is no point in public worship.' Do you agree? Give reasons for your answer, showing that you have thought about more than one point of view.

Research activity

2   What differences can a regular prayer life make to an individual Christian? Try to interview a person for whom prayer is important and try to understand what they experience through prayer.

Summary

You should now be able to explain why and how public and communal worship can help a Roman Catholic to lead a more committed life. You also need to be able to express your own view on this issue.

AQA   Examiner's tip

Remember that you need to know what impact beliefs have on the way people live and feel. It is not enough just to know what they do.

When Christians come together to offer thanks and praise to God as a community they nearly always include selected passages from the Bible. They believe that the Bible is the word of God and that by listening to what God has to say they can come closer to God. The word of Bible is important in helping people to direct their lives (see Chapter 1). However, simply reading the Bible can help Christians to respond to the presence of God. They do not have to do anything; rather they just exist in God's presence.

The Bible itself speaks of the power and importance of the word of God, as in Genesis 1: 'And God said, "Let there be light," and there was light' (Genesis 1:3). This verse shows God's word being outward-going and creative. By listening to it Christians feel that God helps them to become more fully the people he wants them to be. This idea is reinforced in the New Testament when John writes: 'In the beginning was the Word, and the Word was with God, and the Word was God' (John 1:1). The word of God is an outward expression of himself to let people know who he is.

How the Bible is used by different Christian groups

Catholics

In the Catholic Mass there are two main parts: the Liturgy of the Word and the Liturgy of the Eucharist. The Liturgy of the Word usually contains Old and New Testament readings. These are chosen to help believers focus on the way God has guided his people in the past and to learn from these experiences. Over a three-year cycle most of the Bible is read aloud. This allows the whole community to hear what God has shown about himself and to experience, in the sharing of the message, the power of his continuing presence.

Priests in their homilies or sermons (talks) are expected to explain the message of the Scriptures. One of the main functions of a priest is to teach the word of God and this must always be based on the Bible itself.

During the Liturgy of the Word, the central part is the words of consecration: the words of Jesus from the Last Supper that are found in the Bible. Many other prayers during Mass also have their roots in the Bible, notably the Our Father (see pages 94–95).

Protestants

In many Protestant Churches, the services are centred on passages from the Bible. These are often chosen by the minister to focus on a particular theme. These are followed by a sermon in which the minister explains the Biblical passages and shows how their message might affect Christians in their everyday life. The readings and the sermon allow people to understand what God is, how he deals with people and how people should lead their lives. For many Protestant denominations, sharing the word of God has more importance than sharing the Communion celebration (see Chapter 5).

AQA Examiner's tip

Remember that public worship is when the people share prayers and thoughts together, often based on parts of the Bible.

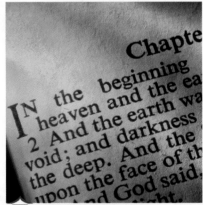

A Christians believe that the Bible is the word of God

links

Look back to pages 10–11 to remind yourself about the Bible as a source of authority for Christians.

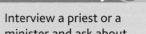

Research activity

1 Interview a priest or a minister and ask about how they use the Bible as the starting point of their sermons.

In **Quaker** services, people come together and sit in silence until one of them feels inspired to speak or to read a particular passage from the Bible. This is seen as passing on the word of God because the person has been influenced by the Holy Spirit to choose the passage for the group.

Some Christians gather together as a **study group**. They read and discuss a particular passage, sharing their thoughts about the meaningfulness and application of that passage to their lives. Each person's insight is shared and explored.

The Psalms (the old Jewish biblical prayers) and other passages from the Bible form the basis of the **Office of the Church**. These are the prayers that all priests, monks, nuns and some lay people say every day, sometimes together, sometimes alone.

B *A minister reading the Bible in church*

Research activity

2 Research how the Bible is used in public worship in one of the Protestant churches or traditions.

∞links

You can find out more about the Psalms on page 92.

Research activity

3 Examine the way in which the Bible is used in the three-year cycle of readings used by many churches.

Extension activity

Open a Bible at random and choose a passage at random. Try to develop a form of service based on this passage. You might use this as the only passage from the Bible or you might decide to use the theme from this passage and find similar ideas to help the service develop.

Activities

1 Explain two ways in which the Bible is used in public worship.
2 Why is the Bible seen as an important source of inspiration in public prayer?
3 'The best way to use the Bible in public worship is to just pick a passage at random.' Do you agree? Give reasons for your answer, showing that you have thought about more than one point of view.

Summary

You should now be able to explain how the Bible is used in public worship and why the Bible is seen as important as the word of God. You should also be able to express an opinion about the value of the Bible in public worship.

The use of the Bible in private worship

Relating to God

As well as being a source of public prayer, the Bible helps individuals when they pray on their own. Many people base their prayers on passages from the Bible. Some people use extracts from the Bible as prompts to help them relate to the presence of God in their lives. By seeing God at work in the lives of others, many believers can find similar situations in which God has helped them. This can be a source of comfort, knowing that God is helping and guiding them. This awareness of the closeness of God can lead people onto a deeper relationship with God.

The teachings of Jesus

The Bible also includes the teachings and example of Jesus, God-made-man, who shows believers the best way to God. By thinking of the events in Jesus' life, many people gain an awareness of how to respond to God themselves. Jesus' constant care for others and his obedience to the Father help them to reflect on the role of God and Jesus in their own lives.

The Psalms

A lot of people pray the Psalms. These are the prayers that Jesus would have used himself. The Psalms are in verse form, like poems. They reflect many different situations that people find themselves in and how these people have found hope in God. For almost every situation in life a psalm can be found that reflects the feelings that that situation inspires. Hope and despair, the joys of youth, the pains of old age and near death, being let down by friends and looking for an answer to the central puzzles of life: all of these situations occur in the Psalms. The Psalms and other similar poetic passages in the Bible can give great comfort and strength. Knowing that you are not alone and that other people have found an answer by turning to God in their time of hope, joy or trouble can encourage people to persevere.

> ### Beliefs and teachings
>
> I lift up my eyes to the hills – where does my help come from?
>
> My help comes from the LORD, the Maker of heaven and earth . . .
>
> The LORD will keep you from all harm – he will watch over your life;
>
> The LORD will watch over your coming and going both now and for evermore.
>
> *Psalms 121:1–2, 7–8*

Other uses

Some people choose a passage from the Bible and use it as a theme for **meditation**. By quietly sitting and reflecting on what that passage means to them that day, they can open their minds and hearts to the presence of God.

Activity

1 Sit quietly and let your thoughts reflect on one short passage from one book in the Bible (it could be a single line). How helpful did you find this exercise? Explain your answer.

A   *Reflecting with a Bible*

Research activities

1   Select ten extracts from the Bible, possibly at random. Ask other people how helpful they find the ideas contained in the extracts you have chosen. (The extracts can be between one and ten verses long but try to ensure that each extract makes sense on its own – there is no point in taking something from the middle of a story that needs the start and ending to make sense.)

2   Ask ten Christians how they use the Bible. Draw up a pie chart or graph to reflect your findings.

Activities

2   Explain what you think are the strengths and weaknesses of each of these uses of the Bible in private prayer.

3   'Christians should just talk to God. They should not depend on the written word of the Bible when they pray.' Do you agree? Give reasons for your answer, showing that you have thought about more than one point of view.

Some open the Bible at random and use the first sentence on which their eyes fall as a guide in **decision-making**. They believe that the God who inspired the choice will also guide them through to the solution of their problem. While this might at first sight seem more about how to live than how to pray, it does show that the individual trusts God. It is this trust and openness to the word of God that will run through their whole prayer life.

Others simply have the Bible near them to remind them of the **closeness of God** in their time of prayer. By holding a Bible, Christians feel that they are as physically as near to God as they can get. The words and guidance give them comfort, remove any tensions and help them to focus on the God whose word they hold.

Extension activity

Compare the way the Jews use their Bible with the way Christians use the Bible in worship. What are the main areas of similarity and of difference?

Summary

You should now be able to explain how the Bible is used in private worship and how the passages from the Bible might inspire Christians in both prayer and action. You should also be able to express an opinion about the value of the Bible in private worship.

4.8 The Our Father

What is the Our Father?

The **Our Father**, also known as the **Lord's Prayer**, is what Jesus gave to his disciples as a form of prayer when they asked him to teach them to pray. Catholics call it the Our Father after the first two words.

It is regarded as the perfect prayer, not simply because Jesus taught it but because it includes all the different types of prayer. It is accepted and used by all Christians, and reflects beliefs on which all Christians are agreed. It is given in Matthew's Gospel (6:9–13) in the Bible.

What follows is a brief commentary on each phrase of the prayer. It shows the different purposes of prayer that are included in the Lord's Prayer and how these words can impact upon Christians.

Our Father, who art in Heaven

In the word 'Father', Christians acknowledge the child-like relationship they have with God. Through prayer they build up this relationship. By accepting that God is in heaven Christians believe that God is both perfect and yet very much involved in their lives. This phrase is a **statement of faith**.

hallowed be thy name

The name of God does not simply refer to what he is called but is a statement of all that he is. Christians pray that God may be accepted as holy. This is a **prayer of worship or praise**.

A *Jesus preaching – stained glass window*

Thy kingdom come, thy will be done
on earth as it is in heaven

The kingdom or the rule of God spreads as people accept what God is and has done for them. People show this by living by his law and trying to do what is pleasing to God. This **petition** involves a change of heart in those who do not yet perfectly follow God's law. This is a form of a

prayer of adoration, accepting what God is and worshipping him, and of intercession or petition, praying that all people will acknowledge God.

Give us this day our daily bread

The nature of the prayer changes at this point as the focus shifts onto human needs. Note the use of 'us' rather than 'me', stressing Christians' relationship with their fellow human beings. In asking for their daily bread, they are seeking the basics for survival, not luxuries. Some Christians also see this as asking for the bread of the Eucharist that will help build them up spiritually in the way normal bread builds them up physically. This is a **prayer of intercession**, asking for the needs of all people.

and forgive us our trespasses as we forgive those who trespass against us

Trespasses are sins and offences. Christians ask God to let them off the effects of what they have done wrong. This is both a **prayer of confession** or **contrition**, being sorry for what they have done wrong, and a **prayer of intercession**, asking for forgiveness. They also promise to share this forgiveness with others.

And lead us not into temptation, but deliver us from evil

Temptations to do wrong are an important element in people's lives. Christians ask God to remove these temptations from their own lives. This is a **prayer of petition**.

Many Christians add an extra phrase to the Our Father, and this phrase is used at Mass shortly after the prayer: 'For thine is the kingdom, the power and the glory for ever and ever.' This is a short hymn of praise to God (called a doxology) which is a Christian's way of accepting all that God has done.

The impact of the Our Father

The Our Father stresses the importance of the community. Its first word is 'our', not 'my', which shows that all Christians are united in Christ and have to work together to maintain this unity. It also means that all people are equal as children of God. Everyone has a duty to bring in God's kingdom by showing others how to live, simply by setting a good example. This includes being willing to forgive when things go wrong and sharing food with those in need.

Activities

2 Explain how four of the phrases in the Our Father might guide the Christian community in its actions.

3 'The Our Father is the only prayer Christians need.' Do you agree? Give reasons for your answer, showing that you have thought about more than one point of view.

Activity

4 What does this case study suggest about the Our Father?

The old lady and the priest

Case study

Father Peter was doing a visiting round in hospital, when a nurse told him that she thought the old lady in a side cubicle was a Roman Catholic. Fr Peter went in and introduced himself and asked if the lady were a Catholic. 'Oh yes, Father,' came the reply. Fr Peter asked if she wanted Communion and the lady said yes. Fr Peter started to say some of the regular prayers and the lady was totally silent. Fr Peter then suggested that they say the Our Father together. The lady started 'Our Father, who art in heaven . . .' and then she stopped. Fr Peter was really worried at this point and was about to stop the service, when the lady apologised. 'I'm sorry, Father, but whenever I get to that point I just can't help thinking of the greatness of God and I forget where I am.' After the prayers were over, Fr Peter went away thoughtfully. He understood that the lady knew a great deal about prayer.

Summary

You should now be able to explain what the Our Father is and how the phrases in the Lord's Prayer might guide the actions and attitudes of Christians. You should also be able to evaluate the impact of the Our Father on individuals and the community.

4.9 Beliefs about Mary

Both the Roman Catholic and the Orthodox Churches have a great respect for the person of Mary. They do not worship Mary; they only worship God. However, because Mary had a very important part to play in the history of salvation, she is greatly honoured by many Catholics.

Mary as the mother of God

The role of Mary is centred on her accepting God's invitation to become the mother of Jesus.

Luke (1:26–38) tells of how the angel Gabriel came to Mary, and announced that Mary had been chosen to bear the Son of God. (This is known as the Annunciation.) Mary questioned how this could be since she was a virgin. The angel told her that God's Holy Spirit would work through her. Mary accepted this with the words, 'I am the Lord's servant. May it be to me as you have said.' In this way Mary accepted all that God wanted from her.

The virgin birth of Jesus points to the fact that Jesus is true God and true man. If he had been born of normal human intercourse Jesus might have been nothing other than human. However, he had to be a human being who lived a life of total obedience to the will of God and defeated evil. Through accepting what God wanted from her, Mary became the mother of God-made-man. Because Jesus is truly God, Mary is honoured by the title **Mother of God**. Catholics believe that to deny her this title would be to say that Jesus was not God-made-man.

As the mother of Jesus, Mary had a special place in Jesus' affection.

Roman Catholics believe that Mary remained a virgin throughout her life, being totally dedicated to the will of God. She is a role model for Christians of what will happen to all those who are faithful to God.

Mary as the Mother of the Church

Mary is the Mother of the Church. This belief is based on the events at Jesus' Crucifixion as recorded in John's Gospel:

Beliefs and teachings

When Jesus saw his mother there, and the disciple whom he loved standing nearby, he said to his mother, 'Dear woman, here is your son,' and to the disciple, 'Here is your mother.' From that time on, this disciple took her into his home.

John 19:26–27

The disciple Jesus loved, traditionally thought to be John, represents all Christians.

A *An icon of Mary with the infant Jesus*

Mary stood by the cross and experienced the pain of her dying son. She accepted all that God requested, without any conditions. In this she is a model of faithfulness.

B   *The Lady Chapel at St Benedict's, Warrington*

Summary

You should now be able to explain why Mary is greatly honoured by Roman Catholics and how they see this honour as stressing the importance of Jesus as God-made-man.

Mary as a role model and guide

Roman Catholics believe that Mary is a perfect human being. They believe that by following her actions and example all believers can reach the perfection that God wants to give them. The following are ways in which Christians might see Mary as a role model and guide, and follow her example and advice.

A life without sin

Mary was conceived without original sin and lived a life without sin. While it might be difficult for Christians to avoid sin, they are called to do their best to live lives pleasing to God.

Commitment to the will of God

Mary accepted the will of God at the Annunciation (Luke 1:26–38). While she could not understand what was happening, she trusted that God would guide her. This total commitment to doing the will of God sets an example that all Christians should try to follow.

Restraint in sexual activity

Mary remained a virgin all her life, according to Roman Catholic teachings. While there is no demand for people to remain virgins, there is a call for Christians to respect their sexuality and to restrict sexual activity to the marriage relationship.

Caring for the needs of others

- Mary went to the help of her cousin Elizabeth who was having her first child in her old age (Luke 1:39–45). This sets an example of caring for the needs of others before focusing on one's own needs.
- At the wedding feast at Cana (John 2:1–12), Mary firstly noticed how the young couple were in trouble and she brought the matter to Jesus' attention. This shows that she was aware of other people and their needs and did what she could do to help in a quiet but effective way. This is how Christians can help other people.

A focus for prayer

Mary is the one who taught Jesus how to pray and how to live according to God's law. In a similar way, Christians look up to Mary as the one to help them in their prayers.

One of the most common prayers used by Roman Catholics is the Hail, Mary.

The first line uses the words of the angel at the Annunciation. The second line uses the words with which Elizabeth greeted Mary. The rest is a plea for help against sin.

Objectives

Examine how Christians can follow the example of Mary.

Understand the relevance of Mary's example for Christians living today.

Evaluate the need to follow Mary's example.

AQA **Examiner's tip**

Remember that you need to show how Mary's example can be followed by Christians. It is not enough simply to know what Mary did.

Beliefs and teachings

The Hail, Mary

Hail, Mary, full of grace, the Lord is with thee.

Blessed art thou among women and blessed is the fruit of thy womb, Jesus.

Holy Mary, Mother of God, pray for us sinners, now and at the hour of our death. Amen.

The perfect mother

Mary is the perfect mother, caring for her child despite the problems that life threw at her. She is therefore an important role model. Christians can similarly protect their own children and help them to grow up as full human beings, in the knowledge and love of God.

Faith in Jesus

At the wedding feast at Cana, Mary told the servants to do whatever Jesus told them to. Her faith in the power and love of Jesus had no limits. Christians should follow this example of trust and also pass on the message to others to respond to the will of God.

Supporting the suffering

Mary stood at the foot of the cross while her son died in great pain (John 19:25–27). It is never easy to support the suffering but Christians are called upon to share with those in any need.

Commitment to prayer

- After the Resurrection, Mary gathered with the Apostles in prayer (Acts 1:14). This shows how prayer has to be a cornerstone of a Christian's life.

- When Mary is reported to have been seen, notably at Lourdes and at Fatima, she always asks people to pray, especially to pray the rosary. Christians could respond to this call wholeheartedly.

A   *Mary with the infant Jesus*

Research activity

1 Find five different occasions when Roman Catholics use the Hail, Mary.

2 Look up each of the passages from the Bible referred to in these pages and write a short account of each of them.

3 Interview ten Roman Catholics and ask them what their opinion is about Mary. Ask them to give you sufficient information for you to draw up a summary of different views about Mary.

Activities

1 Choose three of the examples of Mary's role above and give practical ways in which Christians can follow Mary's example.

2 'If God loves everyone, it will not matter if Christians do not try to be as perfect as Mary.' Do you agree? Give reasons for your answer, showing that you have thought about more than one point of view.

Summary

You should now be able to explain the ways in which Mary might be seen as a role model and guide to be followed by Christians in their everyday life, especially in respect to prayer. You should also be able to evaluate opinions about the importance of Mary.

Extension activity

Compare the way Mary is regarded in the Roman Catholic tradition with the views of other Christian traditions. Why do these traditions hold the views that they do? What is your opinion on these differences?

4

Worship – summary

For the examination you should now be able to:

✔ understand how Roman Catholics practise the faith in both private and public worship

✔ describe different forms of worship: liturgical, non-liturgical, structured and spontaneous; and understand their impact on believers

✔ understand how prayer and meditation and the use of aids to worship help believers in private worship

✔ understand the importance of private worship for the believer

✔ know and understand how the Bible is used in private and public worship

✔ know the Our Father and understand its impact on the individual and the community

✔ know and understand the role of Mary as the Mother of God and her place in Roman Catholic belief as guide and role model

✔ evaluate the importance of each of these topics.

Sample answer

1 Write an answer to the following exam question:

Explain why some Christians believe that meditation is a good form of prayer.

(6 marks)

2 Read the following sample answer.

> Meditation means trying to focus on one thing and block everything else out. You relax so much in meditating that you cannot help but fall asleep.

3 With a partner, discuss the sample answer. Do you think there are other things the student could have included in the answer?

4 What mark would you give this answer out of 6? (Look at the mark scheme in the Introduction on page 7 (AO1) before you attempt this.) What are the reasons for the mark you have given?

AQA Examination-style questions

1 Look at the photograph below and answer the following questions.

(a) Explain how Christians can find help in getting close to God by using:
(i) private prayer
(ii) the rosary.

(6 marks)

(b) 'Public worship is only done to make others think the worshipper is a good Christian.' Do you agree? Give reasons for your answer, showing that you have thought about more than one point of view.

(6 marks)

(c) Explain why the Our Father is important to Christians.

(6 marks)

(d) 'Christians should do their best to follow the example of Mary.' Do you agree? Give reasons for your answer, showing that you have thought about more than one point of view.

(6 marks)

Remember that in each of the question parts above there is one central topic: (a) private prayer, (b) public worship, (c) the Our Father, (d) the example of Mary. Make sure all the material you use within that part of the question is directly relevant. Do not use material that really belongs to another part of the whole question, otherwise you will not be credited for what you know.

5.1 The origins of the Eucharist: the Last Supper

The **Eucharist** is the central service in the Roman Catholic and other Christian traditions. It celebrates Jesus' death and Resurrection using bread and wine. It re-enacts the ceremony Jesus himself performed at the **Last Supper**, the meal he shared with his disciples the night before he died.

Objectives

Know how the Eucharist started in order to appreciate why it is important.

The Last Supper

All the Gospels agree that the Last Supper, which took place on the first night of the Jewish festival of Passover, was an important event for Jesus. Mark's account of the occasion in the Bible is well known:

Key terms

Eucharist: literally 'thanksgiving'. Another name for Holy Communion. Thanks are given to God for his creation of the world, for the life, death and Resurrection of Jesus and for the bread and wine which many Christians refer to as Jesus' Body and Blood.

Beliefs and teachings

The Last Supper

On the first day of the Feast of Unleavened Bread, when it was customary to sacrifice the Passover lamb, Jesus' disciples asked him, 'Where do you want us to go and make preparations for you to eat the Passover?'

So he sent two of his disciples, telling them, 'Go into the city, and a man carrying a jar of water will meet you. Follow him. Say to the owner of the house he enters, 'The Teacher asks: Where is my guest room, where I may eat the Passover with my disciples?' He will show you a large upper room, furnished and ready. Make preparations for us there.'

The disciples left, went into the city and found things just as Jesus had told them. So they prepared the Passover.

When evening came, Jesus arrived with the Twelve . . . While they were eating, Jesus took bread, gave thanks and broke it, and gave it to his disciples, saying, 'Take it; this is my body.'

Then he took the cup, gave thanks and offered it to them, and they all drank from it.

'This is my blood of the covenant, which is poured out for many,' he said to them. 'I tell you the truth, I will not drink again of the fruit of the vine until that day when I drink it anew in the kingdom of God.'

Mark 14:12–17, 22–25

A *The Last Supper – stained glass window*

The Passover meal was the most important event in the Jewish year at the time of Jesus. It remembered the Jews' escape from Egypt, the crossing of the Sea of Reeds and the making of the Covenant at Mount Sinai. It re-enacted and celebrated the fact that the Jews were the people of God.

Jesus wanted to celebrate this meal of friendship before he died. He also wanted to give his followers something by which they could remember him. This is why he gave them the broken bread and poured wine as his Body and Blood. A broken body is a dead body and therefore the disciples were given a share in Jesus' death. Equally, blood that is poured out is also a symbol of death. By giving his Body and Blood to his disciples in this way he was helping them to take part in his death in a real way. Christians believe that by sharing in his death and believing in the Resurrection, the sharing in the broken body also becomes a sharing in Jesus' Resurrection.

A simple parallel might be made here with a normal birthday or wedding party. If people cannot be present at the celebration meal, it is common practice to send them a piece of the cake so that they can still feel a part of the event. Jesus wanted to enable his disciples and those who followed them to have a part in the victory over death and sin that his death and Resurrection would bring about.

B   *A traditional Passover meal in a modern Jewish house*

Research activity

Read Mark chapter 14. Draw up a chart to show the main events that are mentioned in this chapter. Why is the Last Supper important in this chapter?

Activities

1   Either act out the Last Supper as presented by Mark or write a poem about it.

2   Why was the Last Supper important for Jesus?

Extension activity

Find out about the Jewish Pesach (Passover meal), both its origins and the way in which it is celebrated, including the symbols used.

Summary

You should now be able to explain the origins of the Eucharist in the Last Supper.

The origins of the Eucharist: the early Church

Early Christians and the Last Supper

In the early Church, the Breaking of Bread was a regular event. Christians would gather at one person's house, with each person bringing something that they could afford to share. They would eat a meal together and during the meal one of the leaders would repeat what Jesus did at the Last Supper. We have a clear account of this in the Bible in Paul's first letter to the Corinthians:

Beliefs and teachings

Remembering the Last Supper

For I received from the Lord what I also passed on to you: The Lord Jesus, on the night he was betrayed, took bread, and when he had given thanks, he broke it and said, 'This is my body, which is for you; do this in remembrance of me.' In the same way, after supper he took the cup, saying, 'This cup is the new covenant in my blood; do this, whenever you drink it, in remembrance of me.' For whenever you eat this bread and drink this cup, you proclaim the Lord's death until he comes.

Therefore, whoever eats the bread or drinks the cup of the Lord in an unworthy manner will be guilty of sinning against the body and blood of the Lord. A man ought to examine himself before he eats of the bread and drinks of the cup. For anyone who eats and drinks without recognizing the body of the Lord eats and drinks judgment on himself.

1 Corinthians 11:23–29

This passage is important because it comes from one of the earliest New Testament writings. It shows that, right from the start, Christians were coming together to share in the Body and Blood of Jesus. They were fulfilling Jesus' command 'do this in remembrance of me'. Paul, however, also criticised the Corinthians for the behaviour of some of their number. The rich were bringing the food and drink. However rather than wait for the poorer people who could not afford to bring anything, they started to have a feast and get drunk. Paul said that this brought dishonour to the whole Christian community. As the number of Christians grew, there was also the added problem of meeting together in houses big enough to hold them and the practical difficulty of ensuring proper catering. It was easier just to come together to share the central memorial of the Last Supper by sharing the bread and wine, so the meal proper died out slowly.

Objectives

Understand what the early Christians did to celebrate the Risen Christ.

Evaluate whether the early Church's practices are relevant for today.

AQA Examiner's tip

An easy way to think about the Eucharist is to think of the reasons people have celebration meals (not the occasions, but the reasons for those occasions).

Research activity

1 Examine why bread and wine are used as the central symbols of the Lord's Supper. Refer both to the Passover meal and to the symbolic importance of bread and wine for people today.

Activities

1 Explain why the practice of having the Eucharist during a full meal died out.

2 'Times have changed and modern Christians should forget what the early Christians did about celebrating the Eucharist.' Do you agree? Give reasons for your answer, showing that you have thought about more than one point of view.

During the times of persecution under the Roman Empire, Christians would still gather every Sunday, usually in quiet, out-of-the way spots, to celebrate the Eucharist. They would often celebrate the Eucharist near the tomb of someone who had died for the faith (a martyr). This was a sign of the whole Christian community being a witness to Jesus. The Eucharist became the central focus of their worship as it has remained to this day for Roman Catholics.

Persecution of Christians

In many countries Christians are persecuted and the celebration of the Eucharist is often a focus for persecution. In England in the 16th and 17th centuries any priest who was caught saying Mass would be sentenced to death by being hung, drawn and quartered. Women too who gave shelter to priests, such as Margaret Clitherow in York, were killed. In many countries today, similar things are still happening.

Case study

Extension activity

Research the actions of the early Christians during times of persecution. How did they celebrate the Eucharist? What dangers did they face when coming together to celebrate the Eucharist?

Discussion activity

Do you think that celebrating the Eucharist is worth dying for as these people did? Explain your answer to a partner or in a group.

A *Sharing Communion during the Iraq war*

Summary

You should now be able to explain how the early Christians broke bread and shared wine as a remembrance of the Last Supper. You should also be able to evaluate whether this practice is still relevant today.

Research activity

2 Research a place where Christians are persecuted and how this affects the celebration of the Eucharist.

5.3 What is the Eucharist?

The word 'Eucharist' comes from the Greek word *eucharistein*, which means 'to give thanks'. Christians have many things to thank God for: life itself, God's constant love, other people and their love. The most important thing for most Christians is the fact that Jesus, God-made-man, lived and died as a human being to allow all people to enter the eternal happiness of heaven, being with God. The best way for Catholics to express their thanks to God is through the Eucharist that is offered up at every Mass.

The best summary of the Eucharist is, possibly, the prayer written by St Thomas Aquinas for the feast of the Body and Blood of Christ (Corpus Christi):

Beliefs and teachings

O sacred banquet, in which Christ is received; the memory of His Passion is recalled; the soul is filled with grace; and the pledge of future glory is given us.

Thomas Aquinas

This prayer makes the following points about the Eucharist:

- It is a banquet or meal. Christians gather together to share a meal, particularly to recall (or rather to re-enact) the Last Supper that Jesus celebrated with his friends.
- Christ is received. Roman Catholics believe that Jesus is fully present in the consecrated bread and wine. By receiving Communion, Christ enters fully into the life of the individual.
- Christians remember Jesus' suffering and death. At the Last Supper, Jesus gave his disciples the broken bread and the wine as a sign of his death. In this action he helped his followers to be a part of the victory over sin and death that he would achieve by his death and Resurrection.

Objectives

Understand the meaning of the word 'Eucharist'.

Appreciate the importance of the Eucharist for Roman Catholics.

Extension activity

Find out all you can about the celebrations that are associated with the Feast of the Body and Blood of the Lord (Corpus Christi).

Research activity

1 Examine the importance of banquets and meals as places and times of celebrations. In what ways is it useful for Roman Catholics to think of the Mass as a banquet?

 The Eucharistic bread and wine

- The soul is filled with grace. Grace is the free gift of God's life that enables Christians to come closer to God and to bear witness to God in all aspects of their lives.
- The Eucharist is a foretaste of the heavenly feast that Jesus wants all people to share in. What Roman Catholics have now will be fully completed in heaven.

These points are reinforced by the Catechism of the Catholic Church when it says:

Beliefs and teachings

By the Eucharistic celebration we already unite ourselves with the heavenly liturgy and anticipate eternal life, when God will be all in all.

In brief, the Eucharist is the sum and summary of our faith: 'Our way of thinking is attuned to the Eucharist, and the Eucharist in turn confirms our way of thinking.'

Catechism 1326, 1327

Central Roman Catholic ideas about the Eucharist

- It is the best possible way to give thanks.
- It re-enacts the Last Supper, death and Resurrection of Jesus.
- The Eucharist is a shared meal in which Roman Catholics express their common faith.
- Christ is fully present in the bread and wine.
- The Eucharist looks forward to sharing with God and everyone in heaven.

Activities

1   Explain two of the central ideas about the Eucharist.
2   'The Eucharist is so important to Roman Catholics that every Catholic should celebrate the Eucharist every day.' Do you agree? Give reasons for your answer, showing that you have thought about more than one point of view.

A Roman Catholic's view on the Mass

Dorothy is a 66-year-old widow.

'I really like going to Mass because I feel in some deep way that I cannot put into words that Jesus is really present. I feel caught up in what he did when he died and I firmly believe that he enters my life when I receive Communion. It is important to be with other people when I pray to God. When I was in hospital and couldn't get to Mass, my prayer life became less meaningful. Going to Mass has gradually become a central part of my day, even though at times it is difficult. I don't like to miss Mass as my day somehow seems incomplete without it.'

Case study

Summary

You should now understand the meaning of the word 'Eucharist' and be able to explain the importance of the Eucharist for Roman Catholics.

AQA Examiner's tip

The ideas used about the Eucharist are very deep and it is difficult to put them into simple words. You do not have to know the complicated wording, but you do need to understand the central points.

Discussion activity

1   Try to explain to one or two other people what you understand about each of these bullet points.

Research activity

2   Find out how Roman Catholics treat the consecrated bread and wine. Why do they reserve the hosts that are left over after Mass in the tabernacle? Why do they pray in front of the tabernacle that contains the consecrated bread?

Discussion activity

2   With a partner or in a small group, explain what you think about Dorothy's views.

Research activity

3   The case study shows why Mass is important to one Roman Catholic. Talk to Roman Catholics who attend Mass regularly and ask them what they feel about Mass.

There are many different names for the Eucharist, each of which focuses on a slightly different aspect of the sacrament. Each tends to be used by different Christian denominations and often reflects the special importance of the rite for that denomination. However, most denominations are happy to use the majority of the names as there is a great overlap in their appreciation of the ceremony that Jesus left for his followers. The main names used are explained below.

■ Holy Communion

Holy Communion focuses on the idea of eating together. A community was originally a group that shared a common meal. This meal was seen as symbolising everything the people shared (from which idea we get the word community). Even today families, when they get together for a celebration, usually do it in the context of a meal, for example, a wedding feast or a birthday party. When Christians receive the bread and wine they share together in what Jesus shared at the Last Supper.

It is a holy rite because it brings Christians closer to each other and to God through Jesus.

This name is used by Roman Catholics to refer to the moment of receiving the bread and wine. However, it is also used by Anglicans to refer to the whole service in which this ritual takes place.

The Catechism of the Catholic Church says about Holy Communion: 'by this sacrament we unite ourselves to Christ, who makes us sharers in his Body and Blood to form a single body' (1331).

A *What do these Christian symbols show about Christianity?*

Objectives

Know alternative names for the Eucharist.

Understand what each of these names is trying to show about the nature of the Eucharist.

Evaluate the importance of names for the Eucharist.

Key terms

Holy Communion: another name for the Eucharist in which the sacrificial death and Resurrection of Jesus are celebrated using bread and wine.

Mass: another term for the Eucharist, normally used by Roman Catholics. The rite is divided into two parts, the Liturgy of the Word and the Liturgy of the Eucharist.

Lord's Supper: alternative name for the Eucharist or Breaking of Bread.

Breaking of Bread: alternative name for the Eucharist or Holy Communion.

AQA Examiner's tip

Remember that there is much overlap in the ideas contained in each of these names. Just note the different emphasis of each name.

Research activity

1 Find out why each of these symbols is used to represent Christians or Christianity.

The Mass

Mass comes from the final words of the Latin *Ite missa est*, meaning 'Go, you are sent'. The message here is very simple. In the Eucharist, Roman Catholics receive the teachings of Christ in the Liturgy of the Word, and the Body and Blood of Christ in Holy Communion. They are sent out into the world to show other people, through their own words and conduct, what Christ has to offer them. A priest once said to a group of Roman Catholics: 'For some people, you are the only Bible they will ever read.' This means that Catholics have to act in a way that is true to the teachings of Jesus. It is through their actions that other people will learn what Christ has to offer.

The Lord's Supper

The **Lord's Supper** focuses on the fact that when Christians share the bread and wine they are repeating what Jesus did at the Last Supper.

This name is more often used by the non-conformist Churches, e.g. the Baptists and Pentecostalists. They believe that taking part in this ceremony is symbolic of the sacrifice which they know Jesus was about to make after the Last Supper. They believe that, in this way, Christians are taking part in an act of remembering something that happened in the past – something that was important for Jesus and is now important for them.

The Breaking of Bread

The early Christians often used the name the **Breaking of Bread** to describe the ceremony – sometimes as a code name for the shared meal.

For the bread to be shared it needs to be split up or broken. This is a reminder of the action of Jesus before he gave the bread to his disciples, when he said, 'This is my body.' It was common Jewish practice to bless and 'break' bread at a meal. According to Luke 24:13–35 (which describes the disciples' meeting with Jesus on the road to Emmaus after his Resurrection), the disciples recognised Jesus when he broke bread with them. For the early Church, this action reminded them that the Risen Christ was still in their midst.

Activities

2   Which of the names you researched do you think is the most meaningful? Explain your answer.

3   'Christians should keep to the original name of "the Breaking of Bread" for their service.' Do you agree? Give reasons for your answer, showing that you have thought about more than one point of view.

Summary

You should now be able to explain what the different names for the Eucharist are and what is emphasised in the use of these names. You should also be able to express an opinion about the importance of the different names.

Activity

1   Draw spidergrams to show the meaning of each of the names used for the Eucharist.

Research activity

2   Research the name given to the Eucharistic celebration in **ten** different Christian denominations. Note: some denominations may not celebrate the Eucharist at all.

B   *Breaking the bread*

Extension activity

Examine the origins of each of the names for the Eucharist, both the original meaning and the group that first used the name. What further information about the Eucharist have you been able to discover through this activity?

The Roman Catholic celebration of the Eucharist

The Roman Catholic Eucharist is more commonly called the Mass.

The basic structure of the Mass

The basic structure of the Catholic Mass is as follows:

- Introduction, including the penitential rite, prayer of praise and opening prayer.
- The Liturgy of the Word, including readings, the homily and bidding prayers.
- The Liturgy of the Eucharist, including the Offertory, the Eucharistic prayer and the consecration, the Our Father, prayers for peace, and Communion.
- Thanksgiving and dismissal.

Objectives

Know how the Roman Catholic Church celebrates the Eucharist.

Appreciate how important the presence of Christ is in the Mass and how the Mass is seen as a sacrifice and a memorial.

A *An altar and cross, linking the ideas of the Mass and Jesus' death*

B *A priest distributing Communion*

AQA Examiner's tip

It is essential that you know the basic structure of the Mass. You must also be aware of its importance for Roman Catholics.

Research activity

1 Choose one of the four ways in which Roman Catholics believe that Christ is present in the Mass. Find out all you can about that belief: its origin in the Bible, the way early Christians showed that this belief was important to them, how the modern structure of the Mass brings out this belief.

The presence of Christ in the Mass

Roman Catholics believe that Christ is present in the Mass in four different ways:

1 In the consecrated bread and wine, which are the Body and Blood of Christ.
2 In the readings, because Christ is the Word of God and the readings, especially the Gospel, are proclaiming the word of God.

3   In the believers gathered together, in two ways. Firstly as each person is filled with Christ in baptism, and secondly as Jesus promised: 'For where two or three come together in my name, there am I with them' (Matthew 18:20).

4   In the person of the priest, because when the priest pronounces the words of consecration, 'This is my Body' and 'This is my Blood', Christ himself works through the ministry of the priesthood to transform the bread and wine into his Body and Blood.

The Mass as a sacrifice

A **sacrifice** is an offering made to God. The Mass is a sacrifice. Christians offer up to God the same sacrifice that Jesus did when he gave his life on the Cross. As the Catechism of the Catholic Church says, 'The Eucharist is thus a sacrifice because it re-presents [makes present] the sacrifice of the cross' (1366), and 'The sacrifice of Christ and the sacrifice of the Eucharist are one single sacrifice' (1367). The Mass is also a sacrifice of the individual believer as each person gives part of their life to attend Mass and to offer this to God. This is reinforced at the Offertory, when the believers present bread and wine as symbols of everyday life to God. They also give monetary offerings, depending on what they can afford, to help the Church and those in need.

C   *The offertory*

The Mass as a memorial

A **memorial** is usually a reminder of past events. However, in the scriptures 'the memorial is not merely the recollection of past events but the proclamation of the mighty works wrought by God for men' (Catechism of the Catholic Church 1363). This means that: 'The Eucharist is the memorial of Christ's Passover, the making present and the sacramental offering of his unique sacrifice' (Catechism 1362).

Summary

You should now be able to explain what the structure of the Mass is and why the Mass is important as a sign of the presence of Christ.

5.6　The structure of the Mass in detail

Every part of the Mass helps Roman Catholics.

Introduction

The community gathers together in God's name.

- Mass begins with the penitential rite in which Catholics apologise to God and to each other for being sinners.
- A hymn of praise (the Gloria) is said.
- This is followed by a prayer appropriate to the day.

Liturgy of the Word

The Liturgy of the Word, in which Christians listen to the Word of God, consists of the following:

- An Old Testament reading to show how God has guided his people in the past.
- A psalm to thank God.
- A New Testament reading which helps believers to apply Jesus' teaching to their own life.
- A Gospel reading from the four accounts of Jesus' life and teachings in which Jesus, the Word of God made flesh, speaks directly to the believers; by hearing the teachings of Jesus and following his example, believers can ensure that they do what God wants.
- The homily, in which the priest makes the readings relevant to today.
- The Creed, a statement of Christian beliefs which the congregation recite together as a sign of their sharing the one faith.
- The Bidding Prayers, in which Christians ask God to care for all their needs and those of others.

A　*The altar ready for Mass*

Liturgy of the Eucharist

The Liturgy of the Eucharist, in which Christians re-enact the Last Supper, consists of the following:

- **The Offertory**: Here Christians present their gifts, bread and wine to God as symbols of all that life has to offer. Bread is the basic food to show what people need to stay alive. Wine is a celebration drink to show that people offer their joys to God. Money is often offered to share with those in need and for the upkeep of the church.

- **The Eucharistic prayer**: During this prayer Christians give thanks to God for all that he has given to them. The central part of the prayer is the **Consecration** when the priest repeats the words of Jesus at the Last Supper: 'This is my Body.' 'This is my Blood, the Blood of the new and everlasting covenant which will be given up for you so that sins may be forgiven. Do this in memory of me.' At this point Roman Catholics believe that God has accepted their plain offerings of bread and wine and transformed them into something much more precious: the Body and Blood of his Son which God then offers back to the faithful.

- **The Our Father**: Christians join together in the prayer that Jesus gave them as a sign of their oneness in Christ.

- **The sign of peace** (usually a handshake or a kiss to show that people accept each other): This reaffirms that the believers are united in Christ and are ready to share the one bread, the Body and Blood of Christ.

- **Communion**: At this point Christians receive Christ into their lives through the bread and wine. The Roman Catholic practice is to use unleavened bread, usually as a type of wafer. These wafers do not produce many crumbs, so there is no problem about what to do with crumbs that are consecrated but not easily consumed. Red, alcoholic wine is used. As alcohol kills germs, those who wish to do so can receive the Wine from a single chalice (cup).

Thanksgiving and dismissal

After a prayer thanking God for all his goodness to them, Catholics are given a blessing and are sent out to take Christ to others in the way they live their lives: 'Go in peace, to love and serve the Lord.'

Activities

1. Either act out or do a series of drawings of the parts of the Mass.
2. Explain what you think are the two most important parts of the Mass. Justify your choices.
3. 'There are too many parts to the Mass and they confuse Christians.' Do you agree? Give reasons for your answer, showing that you have thought about more than one point of view.

Extension activity

Find out about the ways in which catechumens (people who were taking instruction in the Christian faith) had to leave after the first part of the Mass and were not allowed to attend the Liturgy of the Eucharist in the early Church. What does this show about the Liturgy of the Eucharist?

Research activity

1. Choose any two of the Eucharistic Prayers used at Mass. Compare what they say and their meaning. Find out which of the Eucharistic prayers is most popular with regular church-goers and why.

Discussion activity

Explain to a partner or a small group whether you feel it is necessary to be present for the whole of the Mass or whether attendance at only a certain part of the Mass would be enough.

Research activity

2. Investigate what the Mass was like before 1960 (ask any Roman Catholic over 60 years old) and compare it to how the Mass is celebrated today.

Summary

You should now be able to explain the form of the Roman Catholic Eucharistic celebration (the Mass) and explain which are the most essential parts of this celebration.

The Roman Catholic understanding of the Eucharist

The importance of the Eucharist for Roman Catholics

For many Christians the Eucharist is the centre of their worship. Roman Catholics believe that each time they celebrate the Eucharist they share in the experience of the Last Supper, death and Resurrection of Jesus.

Prayer is an act of self-giving to God. Because of this many Catholics talk about Jesus' death on the cross as his great act of obedience and prayer to God. Each time Roman Catholics celebrate Mass, they join in this greatest prayer. All Christian prayers are simply joining in with this great sacrifice of Jesus. This is why Mass is offered up by priests every day if possible.

Because of the different time zones, there cannot be a moment in which somewhere in the world Mass is not being celebrated. Each time Christians pray they are simply joining in with this ongoing stream of praise.

Jesus told his disciples to 'do this in remembrance of me'. The Greek word for remembrance, or memory, is *anamnesis* (similar to the root for the word 'amnesia'). *Anamnesis* does not simply mean to think of a past event. It means to make this event a reality to oneself.

Roman Catholics believe that when Jesus said the bread was his Body and the wine was his Blood, the bread and wine, while keeping the appearance of bread and wine, actually became the Body, Blood, Soul and Divinity of Christ (i.e. the whole Christ). This is called **Transubstantiation**. Christ is fully present in the Eucharist (the Real Presence). So the bread and wine that Roman Catholics receive at Mass are really the Body and Blood of Christ.

The power to change the bread and wine into Christ's Body and Blood is passed on to every priest at his ordination.

A *At the moment of consecration*

Activities

1   Go through each of the points about the importance of the Eucharist and try to explain them in your own words.

2   'There is nothing special in celebrating the Mass.' Do you agree? Give reasons for your answer, showing that you have thought about more than one point of view.

AQA   *Examiner's tip*

Remember you have to be able to talk about the effects of attending Mass and receiving Communion. It is not enough just to know what happens at the service.

The unifying effects of the Eucharist for Roman Catholics

Since the Mass is a shared meal, one of the main aspects of it is that all people are entitled to an equal share. Christians should work to ensure that everybody has their fair share of the world's goods. It is not acceptable to say that people are eating and sharing together and ignore those in the world who are being starved or exploited. This is one of the reasons why collections for the poor take place during Mass.

Christians believe that Jesus died for all people. As the Mass is a re-enactment of the Last Supper, death and Resurrection of Jesus, it stresses that all people are united. There should be no room in Christianity for prejudice or discrimination.

The Eucharist brings the community together and every Christian has a role to play to ensure that all people of every age and gender are made to feel welcome. Christians should organise events that enable those who would normally feel excluded to become a part of the Church, the Body of Christ, united as they receive the Eucharist. Sharing the Eucharist is the ultimate sign of unity.

⊂⊃ links

Look back to pages 106–107 for more on the importance of the Eucharist.

Discussion activity

Explain to a partner or a small group which of the points about the importance of the Eucharist you think are the most important.

Extension activity

2   Find out what the official teachings of different Christian traditions are about sharing Communion with other Christians.

B   *Receiving the Eucharist*

Summary

You should now be able to explain what the Roman Catholic Church teaches about the importance of the Eucharist for Roman Catholics and how central the Eucharist is to their worship.

The Orthodox understanding and practice of the Eucharist

■ The Orthodox understanding of the Eucharist

The Orthodox Churches have the same understanding of the Real Presence of Christ in the Eucharist as the Roman Catholic Church. They believe that in the Eucharist, heaven and earth are united, and that by receiving the Eucharist, the believer has a share on earth in the meal that will be fully shared in heaven.

■ The Orthodox practice of the Eucharist

Orthodox Christians might celebrate the Liturgy (the service in which the Eucharist is celebrated) daily. However, more commonly it is once or twice a week.

For the Orthodox Churches what takes place on the altar is so holy that the main part of the Liturgy takes place behind a screen called an iconostasis.

At each Liturgy, members of the congregation offer loaves of home-made bread to the priest. Of these, one is used for the actual consecration and Communion, and the others are blessed.

Liturgy of the Word

- The congregation sings hymns and prays.
- There is a reading from the Bible, especially from the New Testament.
- The Book of the Gospels is presented to the people in front of the iconostasis (this is called the Lesser Entrance) before the Gospel is read from behind the screen.
- There might be a sermon or homily.

Liturgy of the Eucharist

- The priest and deacon (his assistant) go through the Royal Doors to receive the offerings of bread and the priest selects one loaf to be consecrated. This is placed on the altar (this is called the Greater Entrance).
- Prayers are said that include the Creed and the Lord's Prayer.
- Behind the closed doors, the priest calls down the power of the Holy Spirit and says the 'words of Institution' (the words Jesus said at the Last Supper).
- The consecrated bread and wine are brought through the Royal

Objectives

Know how the Orthodox Church celebrates the Eucharist.

Understand the importance the Orthodox Church gives to the Eucharist.

∞ **links**

Look back to page 65 to see a photo of an iconostasis.

A *An Orthodox Liturgy*

Doors in the middle of the screen to show to the congregation for them to honour.

- The bread is cut into four parts: one piece is put whole into the chalice, one piece is divided between the priests and deacons, one piece is cut into smaller parts and put in the chalice for Communion. The fourth piece is cut into small parts and left on a dish (it is not consecrated).

- For Communion, the priest brings the consecrated bread and wine through the Royal Doors. Those who wish to receive Holy Communion do so by having the bread soaked in the wine presented to them on a spoon. Every baptised member of the Orthodox Church may receive Communion, even babies. Once the individual has received Communion, they kiss the chalice and their mouth is wiped with a cloth.

- A prayer of thanksgiving is said.

- The non-consecrated loaves are shared between the congregation to take home and share with others who did not attend the Eucharist, not as the consecrated Body and Blood, but simply as blessed bread.

B *Inside an Orthodox church*

Activities

1 Explain in what ways the Orthodox and Roman Catholic beliefs and practices about the Eucharist are the same and in what ways they are different.

2 'Believers should be able to see everything that happens during the Orthodox Liturgy.' Do you agree? Give reasons for your answer, showing that you have thought about more than one point of view.

Summary

You should now be able to explain what happens during an Orthodox Liturgy and what the Orthodox Church believes about the Eucharist.

AQA *Examiner's tip*

You need to be able to give a brief account of the Orthodox Liturgy, especially the ways in which it is different from the Roman Catholic Mass.

Discussion activity

With a partner or a small group, explain your thoughts about the Orthodox practice of holding the central parts of the Liturgy behind a screen.

Research activity

1 Try to interview an Orthodox churchgoer and ask about their feelings about the service. In particular, ask about how much of the Liturgy they actually attend, how they feel about men and women being separate and standing during the Liturgy (if they do at their church), and the type of music that is used during the Liturgy helps them to worship.

Extension activity

Find out all you can about the type of music used in the Liturgy, especially its form and its history.

Research activity

2 Either by using the internet or by interviewing an Orthodox priest or deacon, explore the importance of the Liturgy taking place behind the iconostasis. Write a short article about this topic.

Protestant understanding and practice of the Eucharist

Introduction

One of the main causes of division among Christians from the 16th century to the present day has been about the understanding and the practice of the Eucharist. There is a wide range of opinion among the Protestant traditions about what is experienced in Communion. These range from a position very close, if not identical to, the Roman Catholic belief to a total rejection of the need to celebrate a Eucharist. It would be impossible to give a full description here of all the variations that exist so we will simply look at some typical examples of belief and practice.

The Church of England

The structure of the usual Communion service in the Church of England is almost identical to that of the Roman Catholic Church. However, Anglicans' understanding of what happens is different.

Many Anglicans believe that Jesus is present in the bread and wine in a spiritual way as it is consumed (this is called **Consubstantiation**) but is not present in it otherwise. The idea of consubstantiation is that it is the action of receiving the bread and wine that makes Christ present in Communion. This shared action also brings the community together. Most Anglicans do not accept the idea of transubstantiation as held by the Roman Catholic tradition.

Anglicans celebrate Communion every Sunday and sometimes during the week, perhaps on a saint's day or special occasion. However, they hold other services of worship which do not include the Eucharist. These services focus on readings and psalms from the Bible and may include a sermon, the reciting of a creed, and hymn singing. In theory, Anglicans could attend a regular Sunday service but not attend Holy Communion services. There are no rules within the Anglican tradition that say Communion has to be received (unlike the Roman Catholic tradition). Anglicans only start to receive Holy Communion once they have been confirmed.

The Methodist Church

Methodists see the Eucharist as a memorial of the Last Supper and a reminder of Jesus' death and Resurrection. They do not believe that the bread and wine changes but they believe that Christ is present with them in the sharing of Communion. By remembering the death of Jesus in which he showed his generous love for humans, they believe that they are strengthened and challenged to meet the demands of discipleship.

Methodists tend to celebrate the Eucharist once or twice a month. The celebration of Holy Communion follows the same pattern of words and actions as in the Church of England. For Methodists, like Anglicans, it is the receiving of the bread and wine that is the important aspect rather than the bread and wine itself. Methodists only receive Communion once they have been confirmed.

Objectives

Know the variety of practices and beliefs about the Eucharist that exists within the Protestant tradition.

Understand how the practice reflects the beliefs.

AQA Examiner's tip

You will not be asked about any specific Protestant denomination and its practice of and beliefs about Communion. If you are aware of the general practices and beliefs, you should be able to answer any question set on the Protestant traditions.

links

Look back to page 114 to remind yourself of what is meant by Transubstantiation.

Extension activity

Investigate the differences between transubstantiation and consubstantiation.

■ Baptists and the United Reformed Church

The ordained ministers of these churches lead Communion services once or twice a month.

A Communion service is seen as a memorial of the Last Supper and a reminder of Jesus' words and actions on that occasion. The bread and wine are regarded as symbols by which to remember Jesus and his death and Resurrection. Again, they believe Christ is present in the sharing of bread and wine.

The bread and the wine are often served to members of the congregation, who remain in their seats. Very small individual wine glasses are used. This often means that believers can wait until all are served before they eat the bread and drink the wine together. Some believers feel that this adds to the sense of community.

There is no requirement for members ever to receive Communion. However, anyone who attends a Communion service is welcome to join in receiving the bread and wine. Children may receive a blessing instead.

A   *A Baptist Communion service*

Activities

1   Explain why some Protestant denominations only have Communion occasionally.

2   'It is important to remember what Jesus did at the Last Supper.' Do you agree? Give reasons for your answer, showing that you have thought about more than one point of view.

Summary

You should now be able to explain what happens in both practice and belief during Protestant Communion services.

The impact of the Eucharist on believers and why some Christians do not celebrate the Eucharist

For many Christians the most important aspect of the Eucharist is that it is a sign of unity and belonging. It draws Christians together as they remember Jesus, his Last Supper and his death. By being together, people get great strength and commitment to their faith. Many people find that if their faith is going through a time of doubt, sharing with others, especially in Communion, can help them see things in a new light.

Communion also reminds Christians of the need to share with those who have nothing. This leads many Christian churches to doing work for the developing countries, the homeless and the elderly. They want to share with others following the example of Jesus who gave his life for all people. Christians are called to show love in practice and these actions flow from receiving Communion.

There are some Christians, however, who do not hold Communion services.

■ The Salvation Army and the Quakers

These two Christian denominations are among the few who do not have any Eucharistic celebration at all. Nor do they believe in the need for sacraments.

The Salvation Army

Members of the Salvation Army worship God through reading the Bible, sharing fellowship together and working for those in need.

When they gather together on a Sunday, they sing and play music, share Bible readings, prayers and a sermon. They believe it is important to put their faith into action by going out and caring for people, especially those on the margins of society. Whilst they do not repeat Jesus' actions at the Last Supper, they do follow his example of loving and helping others.

Objectives

Know how the Eucharist guides the actions of believers.

Understand why some Christians do not celebrate a Eucharist.

Evaluate the need for a Eucharist.

AQA Examiner's tip

You may be asked general questions about why some Christians do not celebrate the Eucharist. You will need to know about these Christians and their main beliefs.

Research activity

1 Examine what happens in a Salvation Army service. Investigate the importance of the Salvation Army band in worship.

A *A member of the Salvation Army caring for a homeless person*

Quakers

Quakers assemble on a Sunday and sit quietly, waiting for the inspiration of the Holy Spirit to prompt any individual to say something or to read from the Bible. Their focus is on the direct, personal revelation from God. They feel that other signs are distracting and open to abuse. They feel that the direct guidance from the Holy Spirit will ensure that they do what God wants in the way that God wants. They can follow the example of Jesus by being totally open to God in prayer.

B   *A Quaker meeting*

Activities

1   Explain two different ways in which the Eucharist can inspire Christian actions.

2   Is it more important to celebrate the Eucharist or to work for those in need? Explain your answer.

3   'Christians do not need the Eucharist.' Do you agree? Give reasons for your answer, showing that you have thought about more than one point of view.

Research activity

2   Find out all you can about a Quaker Sunday meeting. If possible, interview a member of the Society of Friends (a Quaker) and ask them about the use of silence and waiting for inspiration.

Extension activity

Find out about the origins of the Society of Friends and why the emphasis has been put on the inspiration of the Holy Spirit rather than sacraments.

Research activity

3   Find out about the work of the Salvation Army in your local area. You might find it useful to start by looking at the Salvation Army's national website, http://www2. salvationarmy.org.uk/

The Salvation Army

Case study

The Salvation Army is one of the largest, most diverse providers of social services in the UK after the Government. Founded in East London in 1865, it now works in 115 countries worldwide.

As a church and registered charity, the Salvation Army demonstrates its Christian principles through social welfare provision. Worldwide there are over 1.6 million members, with programmes including homeless centres, drug rehabilitation centres, schools, hospitals and medical centres, as well as nearly 16 000 church and community centres. The work of the Salvation Army is funded through donations from its members, the general public and, where appropriate, local authority and government grants.

Local Salvation Army church and community centres offer a range of activities and services within their local communities. People can become involved in all sorts of ways, through volunteering with fundraising initiatives, attending church services and helping with local activities.

http://www2.salvationarmy.org.uk

Summary

You should now be able to explain how the Eucharist affects the lives of believers and why some Christians do not celebrate any form of Eucharist. You should also be able to express a view on whether there is a need for a Eucharist.

The Eucharist – summary

For the examination you should now be able to:

✔ understand the centrality of the Eucharist in the Roman Catholic and other Christian traditions

✔ know the different names for the celebration of the Eucharist and the significance of these names

✔ explain different celebrations and understandings of the Eucharist that are found within the Christian traditions, in the Orthodox, Roman Catholic and Protestant traditions, and how these reflect differences of belief and practice

✔ know and understand the reasons why the Eucharist is not celebrated in some traditions

✔ evaluate the impact of receiving the Eucharist on the everyday life of a believer.

Sample answer

1 Write an answer to the following exam question:

Explain how the Orthodox Church celebrates the Eucharist.

(6 marks)

2 Read the following sample answer.

> In the Orthodox church, the congregation is separated from the altar by a screen. The men and women stand on either side of the centre. They have a long service called a Liturgy and the congregation come and go as they please. Women present home-made bread and one of these loaves is selected to be consecrated. The other loaves are taken behind the iconostasis and put on a table near the altar. These will be blessed and shared out at the end of the service. For Communion, those who wish to will receive a piece of bread dipped into the wine and served on a spoon. Orthodox Christians believe that the bread and wine are the Body and Blood of Christ.

3 With a partner, discuss the sample answer. Do you think there are other things the student could have included in the answer?

4 What mark would you give this answer out of 6? (Look at the mark scheme in the Introduction on page 7 (AO1) before you attempt this.) What are the reasons for the mark you have given?

AQA Examination-style questions

1 Look at the photograph below and answer the following questions.

(a)   Explain how members of **one** Protestant tradition celebrate the Eucharist.   *(3 marks)*

(b)   Explain why some Christians do not celebrate the Eucharist.   *(3 marks)*

Note that in question (a) you can choose any Protestant tradition (**not** Roman Catholic or Orthodox) but the tradition you choose must have some form of Eucharistic celebration. For question (b) you are asked to explain about those believers who do not celebrate the Eucharist, e.g. the Salvation Army and Quakers. Note that in (b) you do not have to limit yourself to one tradition. You can make any valid comments that apply to any or all of the traditions that do not celebrate the Eucharist.

(c)   'It is more important for Christians to give to the poor than it is for them to celebrate the Eucharist.' Do you agree? Give reasons for your answer, showing that you have thought about more than one point of view.   *(6 marks)*

Remember that you have to present different points of view, even if you are going to show that one view is totally wrong in your opinion. The marks come for the way you present your argument.

Remember that for most Christians the Eucharist leads to their charitable actions. If they do not serve those in need, they would say that there is no point in receiving the Eucharist.

Festivals

6.1 The liturgical year and Advent

Every year the Roman Catholic Church re-enacts the major events that have shaped Christianity. Through these events the Church remembers how God has guided and protected his people (salvation history). This yearly celebration is called the **liturgical year**. The year starts with the season of **Advent** and ends with the festival of Christ the King. This festival focuses on the end of time, when Christ will judge and reign over all people in the world to come. It takes place on the last Sunday of the Church's year.

The order of the festivals (or feasts) and the seasons is the same each year, though the dating of a major section of the year is variable. The day on which Easter is celebrated depends on the phases of the moon, and there are many festivals whose dates are set in relation to the date of Easter.

Christians celebrate the same cycle of festivals every year. The hope is that the believer will each year become more deeply absorbed in the meaning of the festivals rather than simply repeating the same events year after year.

The sections of the liturgical year

The liturgical year can be divided into five main sections:

1 **Advent**.
2 **Christmas** and **Epiphany**.
3 **Lent**, including **Holy Week**.

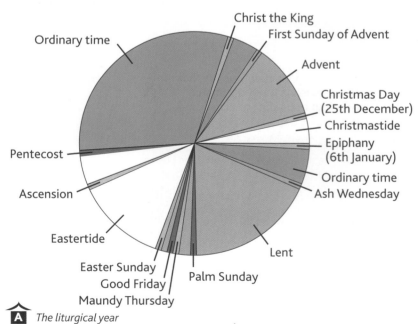

A *The liturgical year*

Labels on the diagram: Ordinary time; Christ the King; First Sunday of Advent; Advent; Christmas Day (25th December); Christmastide; Epiphany (6th January); Ordinary time; Ash Wednesday; Lent; Palm Sunday; Maundy Thursday; Good Friday; Easter Sunday; Eastertide; Ascension; Pentecost

4 **Easter**, including **Pentecost**.

5 Ordinary time when Christians reflect on the growth of the Church and the work of God in people's everyday lives.

Advent

Advent means 'coming'. This festival focuses on two different aspects of salvation:

1 The coming of Christ into the world at the Annunciation (25 March) and at Christmas (25 December).

2 The Second Coming of Christ at the end of time, when he will come in power to judge the living and the dead.

Advent begins four Sundays before Christmas (between 27 November and 3 December). During Advent the readings reflect God's promises of hope and salvation to the Jews. These readings help Christians to prepare for the coming of God's anointed one, the promised Messiah (Christ). The priest wears purple vestments (clothes) during the festival as a sign of preparation and change.

Many people forget about the Second Coming and its relationship with Advent. This theme dominates the first part of the season, taking up the theme of the end of time from the end of the Church's year, the festival of Christ the King.

The last eight days of Advent look forward to the imminent celebration of Christmas and the need to be ready to greet Jesus' coming into the world as a human being. The last day of Advent is 24 December, Christmas Eve.

Most churches light a candle in an **Advent wreath** each Sunday in Advent. An Advent wreath is a circle that holds four candles (usually three purple and one pink), often with a white candle in the centre that is lit on Christmas Day. The wreath is made of evergreen leaves to reflect the abiding love of God for humanity. The increasing light week by week reflects the approach of Jesus, the Light of the world. The third candle tends to be pink rather than purple to reflect a period of joy during the time of preparation; this joy is based on the closeness of Christ.

B *An Advent wreath*

Extension activity

Choose one of the Old Testament readings used during the Advent season. Explain in your own words what this reading means and why it is suitable for the season of Advent.

Research activity

1 Research the dates on which each of these festivals fall this year. There are some useful websites to help with this, for example http://catholicism.about.com/

AQA   Examiner's tip

Focus on Advent as a time of preparation.

Research activity

2 Examine the origin and meaning of one of the symbols used in church during the Advent season.

Activities

2 In your own words, explain what the season of Advent is and why it is important for Christians.

3 'For Christians the Second Coming of Jesus is much more important than his birth as man.' Do you agree? Give reasons for your answer, showing that you have thought about more than one point of view.

Summary

You should now be able to explain how the liturgical year helps Christians to become more deeply aware of the events of salvation history and how Advent is a time of preparation for both the first and the second coming of Christ. You should also be able to express an opinion on the importance of the liturgical year and Advent.

Christmas

Christmas Day is 25 December. This day celebrates the Incarnation. Christians believe that God became a human being in the person of Jesus. God the Son took on the limitations of the human race out of love for each and every person. The birth stories, especially Luke's account of the birth and the visit of the shepherds (Luke 2:1–20), show how Jesus was born as a weak baby, as an outsider. This shows how God cares for all people and how God was prepared to undergo everything that can be experienced by human beings, including poverty and rejection.

Midnight Mass

The festival starts with what is often referred to as **Midnight Mass** (though sometimes it takes place earlier in the evening). The main reason for this Mass being held in the darkness is that Jesus, the Light of the world, has broken the darkness of sin (a theme strongly reinforced at the celebration of Easter). In some churches there is a ceremony of readings and carols before the Midnight Mass begins. The readings are particularly taken from the Old Testament to show how God promised that he would send a Saviour. The first chapters of both Matthew's Gospel and Luke's Gospel give accounts of the events that led up to the birth of Jesus. Parts of these chapters are often included among these readings. Carols are hymns that are specially sung at Christmas and they focus on the birth of Jesus.

To help celebrate the birth of Jesus (the **Nativity**), a **crib** is blessed. This is a representation of the stable scene (usually in statue form). It is a reminder of the story of Jesus' birth told by Luke, when Jesus was born in a stable (a symbol of poverty), among the poorest of people, and was visited by shepherds.

Other celebrations

There are other symbols used which have less religious significance, such as the evergreen tree to show God's eternal love. This is usually brightly decorated with tinsel and other decorations and covered with lights. This shows that darkness has been overcome by God's love.

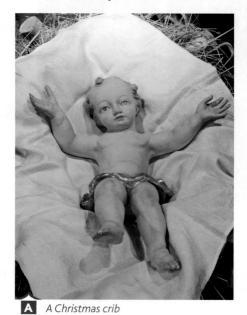

A A Christmas crib

Key terms

Christmas: the Feast Day commemorating the birth of Jesus (25 December).

Midnight Mass: the first Mass of Christmas, showing how Jesus brought light into the dark.

Crib: model of a stable, showing the scene of Jesus' birth.

Epiphany: literally 'appearance'. It is a Christian festival held on 6 January in celebration of Jesus as the Messiah and the Son of God. On the feast of the Epiphany, Christians remember the visit of the Magi (the three Wise Men).

Family celebrations and present-giving are a reflection of the generosity and closeness of God shown in this festival. To increase the special nature of this celebration as a family event, homes are usually decorated, making use of lights in a big way. The family usually come together and have a special meal to reflect that they share the love for each other. This is the love that God has shown for everybody through the birth of his Son. One of the main ways people spread the love of God during the Christmas season is by sending Christmas cards. These enable people to keep in touch with friends who are at a distance and yet who can be made aware of the fact that they are not forgotten.

Epiphany

Traditionally, **Epiphany** is celebrated on 6 January. In England it is now celebrated on the Sunday after 1 January. 6 January is the 12th day of Christmas. It completes the main Christmas celebration.

Epiphany means 'revelation' or 'showing'. The main idea of the festival is to remember the visit of the Wise Men (Magi) to Jesus in Bethlehem, as told in Matthew 2:1–12. This story focuses on the fact that Jesus came to save all people, non-Jews as well as Jews. In the Orthodox Church the feast of Epiphany is more important than Christmas. In some countries, including Spain, presents are exchanged on 6 January, copying the example of the Wise Men, who gave gold, frankincense and myrrh to Jesus.

The festival reflects God's love for all men, a love that should be shared between all people.

B *The three wise men*

Discussion activity

With a partner or in a small group, explain whether you think Christmas is the most important festival of the year, giving reasons for your opinion.

Extension activity

Compare the Gospel birth stories of Matthew chapters 1 and 2 and Luke chapters 1 and 2 with each other and with the stories often told about the birth of Jesus.

Activity

1 'Christmas celebrations should only take place in church.' Do you agree? Give reasons for your answer, showing you have thought about more than one point of view.

Activities

2 Create a Christmas card that includes some religious information about the festival and its importance.

3 Explain why the following family activities can be seen to reflect the religious meaning of Christmas and the Epiphany:

a Exchanging gifts

b Putting up decorations

c Having a special family meal.

Summary

You should now be able to explain how Christmas celebrates the Incarnation, when God became man, and how Epiphany celebrates the revelation of God's love to all people. You should also be able to weigh up different views about the importance of the Christmas season.

Lent

Lent is the 40-day period leading up to Easter. It is a reminder of the period of preparation Jesus spent in the desert before he began his ministry. It is a time when Christians are asked to reflect on their lives, to review the direction that their lives are taking and to make changes if necessary. The lengthy period of Lent helps Christians to prepare themselves to join in the great victory over sin and death, which is celebrated at Easter.

During Lent, priests wear purple vestments as a sign of sorrow and preparation.

The first day of Lent is **Ash Wednesday**, which is a day of fasting and abstinence. Many churches participate in the **distribution of ashes**. Ashes, made from burned palm branches, are used to mark a cross on the believers' foreheads. The ashes are a sign of the person turning from sin and believing the Gospel. They are also a sign of the shortness of life and the belief that people will have to face death and judgement eventually.

To help Christians use the time of Lent productively and to prepare to celebrate the Easter season, Christians are encouraged to take on extra spiritual exercises, especially prayer, **fasting** and **works of mercy**.

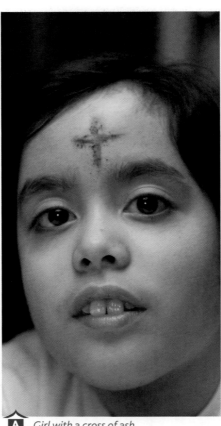

A *Girl with a cross of ash*

Objectives

Examine what is celebrated during the season of Lent.

Understand how the practices and services of this time help Roman Catholics to get more involved in this season.

Evaluate the importance of this season.

Key terms

Lent: the 40-day period before Easter, in which Christians are called to pray, fast and give to charity in preparation for Easter. It recalls the 40 days that Jesus spent in the wilderness after his baptism.

Ash Wednesday: the first day of Lent, a time of penitence. People come to church on this day and have the 'sign of the cross' marked on their foreheads with ashes.

Distribution of ashes: people come to church on Ash Wednesday and have the 'sign of the cross' marked on their foreheads with ashes. The ash is a reminder that human beings only have a brief time on earth and a sign that they are really sorry for their sins.

Fasting: people fast during Lent as a way of preparing for Easter. Fasting helps Christians to focus on what they really need for survival.

Works of mercy: works of mercy are intended to help those people who are in need. Lent can help Christians to share what they have with those people who are worse off than themselves. It is a way of helping Christians to get a right balance in life towards possessions.

Activities

1 Explain the significance of putting ashes on the forehead on Ash Wednesday.

2 Explain why Lent is 40 days long.

Research activity

1 Ask 20 people how they feel about the practice of having ashes on their forehead on Ash Wednesday. Produce a chart or graph to plot their answers.

- **Prayer** helps a Christian to come closer to God. By praying more during the season of Lent, Christians are focusing on their relationship with God. The quality of prayer as well as the quantity should improve, to help Christians remember how important God is in their lives.

- **Fasting** helps Christians to focus on what they really need for survival as opposed to luxuries. They attempt to get rid of the 'extras' in life, the things that can often distract people from what is essential. In this way Christians can use Lent as a way of sorting out their relationship with themselves re-establishing their own values. It helps to re-establish the really important things in life. This also helps people to become more self-disciplined because it takes effort to carry on doing things you would rather not do for this length of time.

- **Works of mercy** are intended to help those people who are in need. The works of mercy are the actions for which Jesus praised those who were to be rewarded by a place in heaven (Matthew 25:31–46): to feed the hungry, give drink to the thirsty, clothe the naked, visit the sick and those in prison and welcome the stranger. Lent can help Christians to share what they have with those people who are worse off than themselves. This can be done by personal direct care or by fundraising to send to those in need, for example refugees. It is a way of helping Christians to achieve the right balance in life towards possessions.

The three practices of prayer, fasting and works of mercy together can help Christians to sort out their relationships with God, themselves and other people. As a result, by the time Easter comes, they are on the right course and they can continue living good, Christian lives.

Examiner's tip

The main focus of Lent is to prepare for Holy Week and Easter. Prayer, fasting and works of mercy are three ways in which this may be done.

Research activity

2   CAFOD has one of its family Fast Days early in Lent. Research how this event fits in with the spirit of Lent.

Discussion activity

With a partner or in a small group, explain whether you think Lent is a challenge and a challenge that is worth responding to.

Case study

The challenge of Lent

Anne is a 35-year-old mother who is a committed Christian.

'I like Lent. This is not being morbid but Lent challenges me. I know my life can drift too easily. Lent helps me to think about where I am going. It is only for 40 days, so I can encourage myself with the short-term goal. Easter is a good point to reach, knowing that I have done what I set out to do. OK there are many slips on the way, but I don't just give up and call my efforts hopeless. The most encouraging part about Lent is that when things get really bad I remember that Jesus had to struggle on his way to Calvary but he didn't give in.'

Activities

3   Explain how the practices of prayer, fasting and works of mercy might help Christians.

4   'Christians should not need to celebrate Lent every year.' Do you agree? Give reasons for your answer, showing that you have thought about more than one point of view.

Extension activity

Choose one of the readings used during Lent. Explain in your own words what this reading means and why it is suitable for Lent.

Summary

You should now be able to understand the importance of Lent for Christians, especially in following the example of Jesus in the desert, and to explain how this festival is celebrated. You should also be able to explain your views about the importance of Lent.

The last week of Lent is called **Holy Week**, when Christians remember and re-enact the events of the last week of Jesus' life. During Holy Week the Mass and the readings tend to be very specific, notably the use of the Suffering Servant poems of Isaiah (42:1–9, 49:1–6, 50:4–9, 52:13–53:12). There is a lot of symbolism used, for example, palm branches and kissing the Cross.

Holy Week includes the following celebrations:

- **Palm Sunday**
- **Maundy Thursday**
- Good Friday
- Holy Saturday.

Maundy Thursday, Good Friday and Holy Saturday are sometimes collectively referred to as the Easter Triduum (three days).

Palm Sunday

This is the Sunday at the beginning of Holy Week. It is also known as Passion Sunday.

Mass starts with a blessing of palms (tree branches that were waved as a sign of greeting) and the reading of the Triumphal Entry of Jesus into Jerusalem from Mark's Gospel.

A *Palm crosses*

This is followed by a procession with the palm branches. This reminds people of the great welcome given to Jesus as the Messiah at the start of his mission in Jerusalem. Many Christians see this event as the first step leading up to the death of Jesus.

Beliefs and teachings

As they approached Jerusalem . . . [when some disciples] brought [a] colt to Jesus and threw their cloaks over it, he sat on it. Many people spread their cloaks on the road, while others spread branches they had cut in the fields. Those who went ahead and those who followed shouted,
    "Hosanna!"
    "Blessed is he who comes in the name of the Lord!"

Mark 11:1, 7–9

During the Mass, the readings focus on the suffering and death of Jesus, the **Passion**, for example Mark 14:1–15:47.

Maundy Thursday

This day is the day before Jesus died.

The **Mass of the Lord's Supper** is usually celebrated at 7.30 p.m. thought to be roughly the time that the Last Supper (the first Mass) took place. The Mass commemorates three different aspects of Jesus' last meal with his disciples:

1 When Jesus washed the disciples' feet and gave them a new command (mandatum) to love one another. The priest re-enacts the **washing of the feet** by washing the feet of 12 parishioners.

B *Jesus washing the disciples' feet*

2 When Jesus broke the bread and gave the wine as his Body and Blood to be given up for all people. This is the **institution of the Eucharist**, the first Mass that is re-enacted at every Mass.

3 The command to 'do this in memory of me'. This is seen as the institution of the priesthood, as at every ordination the power to re-enact the Last Supper at Mass is given to the new priest. What the priest does at Mass is exactly what Jesus did at the Last Supper.

When the Mass is over, the consecrated bread is taken in procession to the **Altar of Repose**, a side chapel set aside for private prayer. This commemorates Jesus going to the Garden of Gethsemane to pray. People are encouraged to pray privately before the Blessed Sacrament in the Altar of Repose until midnight to reflect on Jesus' agony in the garden and his arrest.

The main altar is stripped bare, to reflect the desolation of Jesus at his arrest and trial.

Discussion activity

With a partner or in a small group, explain which of the above three aspects of Maundy Thursday you think is the most important.

Activities

1 Explain what Palm Sunday commemorates and why Palm Sunday is the start of Holy Week.

2 'There are too many different events recalled in the Maundy Thursday ceremonies to allow Christians to do any of them properly.' Do you agree? Give reasons for your answer, showing that you have thought about more than one point of view.

Summary

You should now be able to understand the importance of Palm Sunday and Maundy Thursday for Christians and to explain how these festivals are celebrated. You should also be able to evaluate the importance of the different events on Maundy Thursday.

Key terms

The Mass of the Lord's Supper: Christians share in the same meal – just as Jesus' disciples did at the Last Supper. This term is more often used by the Free Churches (Baptists, and Pentecostal Churches, etc.) by doing exactly as Jesus did.

The washing of the feet: usually 12 parishioners sit at the front of the church and have their feet washed by the priest during the Holy Thursday Mass, a reminder that Jesus washed the feet of his disciples in the Upper Room at the Last Supper. Jesus gave the disciples a new command (mandatum) to love one another.

The institution of the Eucharist: at the Last Supper Jesus gave his disciples bread and wine to represent his body and blood. This is the institution of the Eucharist (the first Mass) that is re-enacted at every Mass. Jesus commanded his disciples to 'do this in memory of me' i.e. the institution of the priesthood.

The Altar of Repose: when the Mass is over on Holy Thursday, the consecrated Bread is taken to the Altar of Repose. This is a side chapel set aside for private prayer to remember Jesus going to the Garden of Gethsemane to pray. People pray privately at this Altar to remind them of the agony of Jesus in the garden and his arrest.

Good Friday

Good Friday recalls the trial, the sufferings and the death of Jesus. It is called 'Good Friday' as the focus is on all that Jesus accepted because he loved all people. By sinning, human beings had separated themselves from God. Jesus came on earth and never did anything against the will of God. His agony in the garden of Gethsemane before his arrest (remembered on Maundy Thursday) was because Jesus had to make a life and death decision: should he stay in the garden and be arrested and killed or should he run away and live on, rejecting what God wanted?

A   *Jesus on the Cross*

He stayed and did nothing to prevent his death from happening. He did not defend himself against false charges at his trial. He endured the whipping and the mockery that took place after the trial. He had to carry the cross through the mocking crowd (the contrast with the cheering crowd on Palm Sunday is symbolic of his total rejection by the people he came to save). His slow, painful death by crucifixion was a public event. This was a guarantee that Jesus actually died since no criminal was allowed to escape death. He was buried by a good Jew, not one of his close friends.

There is only one important service on Good Friday and it takes place at 3.00 p.m., the time when Jesus died on the Cross.

There is no Mass on this day but the service has a set format:

- The **readings**, especially the reading of the Passion and death of Jesus found in John's Gospel (John 18:1–19:42). This helps Christians to reflect on what this day is remembering.

- The **Bidding Prayers**, a long series of prayers asking for God's help for the Church, the world and all people, believers and non-believers alike.

- The **Adoration** (or **Veneration**) **of the Cross**: a Crucifix is processed though the church, often being uncovered during the procession. Then people come and kiss the Cross as a sign of accepting the salvation Jesus won for all people.

Objectives

Understand the importance of Good Friday and Holy Saturday for Christians.

Appreciate how the ceremonies of Good Friday help Christians to remember the events celebrated.

Evaluate the need for Good Friday ceremonies.

AQA Examiner's tip

Remember that the whole focus on Good Friday is the suffering and death of Jesus – everything else just reinforces this point.

Key terms

Good Friday: the Friday before Easter, when Christians remember the crucifixion and death of Jesus.

The Adoration of the Cross: an act of devotion. On Good Friday a wooden cross is laid in front of the congregation and each person comes forward to kiss it.

United service of witness: all the Christian Churches have a united service on Good Friday, often carrying a cross in procession through the main streets. This reminds all people to thank Jesus for the death he suffered for all mankind.

- **Communion**: The Blessed Sacrament (the consecrated bread) is brought from the Altar of Repose for believers to receive Communion in the form of bread alone.

In many towns all the Christian churches have a **united service of witness**, often carrying a cross in procession though the main streets. This is a witness to all people of Christians thanking Christ for the death he suffered.

Many people attend a service based on the **Stations of the Cross**. This is a service in which believers symbolically follow the journey of Jesus from Pilate's house to Calvary and to the tomb by reflecting on 14 episodes on the journey. There are 14 plaques on the walls of the church and prayers are said at each of these plaques. This helps the believers to unite with Jesus in his sufferings.

Holy Saturday

Holy Saturday commemorates Jesus in the tomb, among the dead. The church is bare this day and no sacraments may be received.

B   *One of the Stations of the Cross*

Key terms

Stations of the Cross: a service that remembers the journey of Jesus from Pilate's house to the tomb. It takes place throughout Lent (and at other times), as well as on Good Friday.

Activities

1. Why is Good Friday called 'Good Friday'?
2. Explain the importance of the reading from John's Gospel and the Veneration of the Cross on Good Friday.
3. 'Good Friday should not be treated as a special day by Christians.' Do you agree? Give reasons for your answer, showing that you have thought about more than one point of view.

Extension activity

1. Examine the arguments for and against celebrating Mass on Good Friday.

Research activities

1. Read the Passion story according to John (18:1–19:42). Write out a diary of the events that John relates.
2. Interview three Christians and ask them what religious services or events they normally attend on Good Friday. Find out what these services mean to them.

Summary

You should now be able to understand the importance of Good Friday and Holy Saturday for Christians and to explain how these festivals are celebrated. You should also be able to evaluate the need for special ceremonies on Good Friday.

Extension activity

2. Using the internet find out about what Christians think about on Holy Saturday and how this has affected the nature of any celebrations on this day. You might find one of the following websites useful:

http://lent.goarch.org/holy_saturday/learn/

http://www.churchyear.net/holysaturday.html

http://www.ewtn.com/faith/lent/Holy_sat.htm

The Easter Vigil

Easter is the celebration of the Resurrection of Jesus from the dead. The Easter season starts with the **Easter Vigil** service and lasts for 50 days, until Pentecost.

One of the earliest decisions that the Church had to make was when to keep the feast of Easter. Some Christians wanted it celebrated on the date Jesus rose, regardless of the day of the week. But the majority preferred to celebrate Easter on a Sunday. The decision was that Easter should fall on the Sunday after the full moon after the spring equinox (21 March). This means that the date of Easter moves each year.

The Easter Vigil

The Easter Vigil ceremony takes place after nightfall between the Saturday and the Sunday. Some churches still hold the practice of starting the Vigil about 11.00 p.m. so that the Mass of Easter itself starts just after midnight.

One of the great symbols used is that of light. Light represents the Resurrection breaking the darkness of sin and death and bringing new light. There are two forms of light used: firstly, a (usually small) bonfire that should be lit by flint; secondly, a light is taken from the fire and used to light the **Paschal** (Easter) **candle**. This candle is used throughout the year as a symbol of the Risen Christ.

The Easter Vigil ceremony has different stages that are full of symbolism, reflecting the importance of the Resurrection of Jesus and the new life of the believers.

- The lighting and blessing of the new fire. The fire symbolises new light and life, breaking through the power of darkness and sin.
- The lighting and blessing of the Paschal candle. There is a procession of the Paschal candle through the church during which

A *Lighting a candle from the Paschal Candle*

Key terms

Easter: the religious season celebrating the Resurrection of Jesus from the dead. It starts on Easter Sunday and finishes with the feast of Pentecost.

Easter Vigil: the Roman Catholic main celebration of Easter is on Holy Saturday.

Paschal Candle: the candle which is lit on Holy Saturday to symbolise the light of Christ's Resurrection.

Discussion activity

With a partner or in a small group, discuss whether Easter Sunday should be on a fixed date.

Research activity

1. Examine all the markings that are used on a Paschal candle and explain the meaning of each of them. Draw up your own design for a Paschal candle, using the information you have researched.

every member of the congregation is given a light from this candle. The gradual increase of light in the church as each person receives a lighted candle shows the spread of the light of Christ in the world as the religion increases.

- This is followed by a great hymn of praise to God for the gifts of this day. This shows how Christians are called to walk in the light of the Risen Christ that is symbolised by this candle.

- There is a series of readings. The readings focus on how God (a) created the world, (b) saved the Jews from Egypt and (c) wants to work through his people to recreate his relationships with the whole earth. This challenges believers to reflect on their own relationship with God.

- The Gloria and the Easter Alleluia, which proclaim the Resurrection. The word Alleluia (which means 'praise the Lord') is not said throughout Lent – it is saved for use as a celebration of the Easter message. The Easter Alleluia is the great hymn of victory.

- The readings of the Mass focus on the importance of the Resurrection. The Gospel reading is an account of the discovery of the empty tomb that led to the resurrection appearances by Jesus and the belief in the Risen Christ that is central to Christianity.

- The blessing of baptismal water. Water is a sign of both death and life. Jesus has been through the waters of the tomb and has given new life to all people. Any new converts to Roman Catholicism are received into the Church at this point.

- The renewal of the baptismal promises, showing that the believers accept the life of the Risen Lord into their own lives.

The rest of the Mass follows as normal.

B *Baptism is an important symbol of the Easter Vigil*

Activities

1. Explain why the Easter Vigil is celebrated after nightfall.
2. Explain why the Easter Vigil is a good time to receive new converts to the Church.
3. 'The Easter Vigil is the most important ceremony in the Church's year.' Do you agree? Give reasons for your answer, showing that you have thought about more than one point of view.

  Examiner's tip

Remember how powerful the idea of light breaking the darkness is as it symbolises all that Christians believe about the Resurrection.

Research activity 🔍

2 Examine the symbols of light and water that are used during the Easter Vigil and explain their importance.

Extension activity

Show the meaning and significance of any three of the readings chosen for the Easter Vigil.

You can choose from the following:

Genesis 1:1–2:2, 22:1–18

Exodus 14:15–15:1

Isaiah 54:5–14, 55:1–11

Baruch 3:9–15, 32–4:4

Ezekiel 36:16–28

Romans 6:3–11

Matthew 28:1–10 (or Mark 16:1–8 or Luke 24:1–12)

Summary

You should now be able to understand the importance of the Easter Vigil and the symbols used during it, especially the symbols of light and water. You should also be able to evaluate the importance of the Easter Vigil.

Easter Day

On **Easter Day**, or **Easter Sunday** as it can also be called, Christians continue to celebrate the Resurrection of Jesus, with great joy and renewed commitment. The Mass of the day is the normal Mass with readings telling of the Resurrection of Jesus, particularly John 20:1–9. The whole feel of the day is one of great joy and rejoicing. The most noticeable change during the Mass is that the congregation does not recite the Creed as a joint statement of faith. Instead all the members of the congregation together renew their baptismal promises and make the sign of the cross on themselves, using the water that was blessed during the Easter Vigil. This shows that all the faithful accept the power of Christ's Resurrection in their own lives. At every Mass throughout the Easter season, the Paschal Candle is lit as a sign of the presence of the Risen Christ with his people.

A   A Paschal Candle

Ascension

Ascension takes place 40 days after Easter (traditionally on a Thursday). It commemorates Jesus returning to heaven for the last time after having shown himself to his disciples on occasions after the Resurrection. This event is recorded in Acts 1:1–11, which is used for the first reading of the Mass. Christians believe that the Ascension shows that Jesus is alive and reigning with God the Father and the Holy Spirit, nevermore to die, and offering to believers the joys of his Kingdom.

Pentecost

Pentecost takes place 50 days after Easter and completes the Easter celebration. It commemorates the day on which the Apostles received the Holy Spirit (Acts 2:1–12). After the Ascension, the Apostles followed Jesus' instruction to wait in Jerusalem for the coming of the Holy Spirit. On the day of Pentecost, they heard a strong wind and saw flames of fire coming to rest on the head of each of them. The apostles were filled with courage and went out and preached about Jesus being the Lord and Saviour.

This day is the 'Birthday of the Church' because from this day all believers have been given the power to bear witness to Jesus in what they say and do both as individuals and as a community.

Objectives

Know the importance of the Easter season for Christians.

Understand how the Easter season helps Christians to celebrate their faith.

Evaluate the importance of Pentecost.

links

Look back to page 134 for an explanation of what the Paschal Candle is.

Key terms

Easter Day: the day when the Resurrection of Jesus is celebrated by Christians.

Easter Sunday: another term for Easter Day.

Ascension: the event after the Resurrection, when Jesus returned to God, the Father, in heaven, recorded in Luke 24 and Acts 1. The festival commemorating this event is traditionally held on a Thursday 40 days after Easter.

Pentecost: festival 50 days after Easter, remembering the day, shortly after the Ascension, when the Apostles felt the presence of the Holy Spirit (recorded in Acts 2:1–4).

links

You can find out more about what happened on the first Pentecost on page 48.

Activity

1   Read the three passages that are referred to in the text (John 20:1–9, Acts 1:1–11, Acts 2:1–12) and write a short summary of what happens in each passage.

Pentecost reminds Christians of the transforming power of the gifts of God, as the Holy Spirit was able to take fearful people and make them strong in faith and courage. It is a sign that everything is changed through the power of God's Spirit. This gift is available to everyone who accepts Jesus as Lord.

The importance of Easter

Easter makes sense of everything that Christians go through for the rest of the year. There would be no point in the Birth of Jesus without his Death and Resurrection. The disciplines of Lent and the awkward timings of the ceremonies during Holy Week all have a purpose if you see them in the light of Jesus' victory over death. Too many people see religion as a gloomy thing and think that Christians, and especially Roman Catholics, always have long faces and boring services. However, the Resurrection shows that there is always hope. No matter how bad things appear, God can transform them. Jesus' triumph over death means that there is nothing to be afraid of in death. People might not like the process of dying, but Jesus' own death was difficult too. The beauty of Christianity is the promise that death is not the end. This means that all Christian funeral services should have some hope and joy, even though people are sad to be separated from their loved one. The dead person has joined Christ in his victory over death and will hopefully join Christ in heaven.

Case study

Discussion activity

With a partner or in a small group, explain what you think about the thoughts expressed in this case study.

AQA Examiner's tip

Make sure you understand the importance for Christians of the three festivals mentioned here.

B   *The Holy Spirit pictured as a dove*

Activities

2   Explain how the three festivals of Easter, Ascension and Pentecost are linked together.

3   'Christians should pay more attention to the feast of Pentecost than they currently do.' Do you agree? Give reasons for your answer, showing that you have thought about more than one point of view.

Summary

You should now be able to explain the importance of the Easter season and how the Easter season is celebrated by the Roman Catholic Church. You should also be able to evaluate the importance of Pentecost for Christians.

6

Festivals – summary

For the examination you should now be able to:

✓ know and understand the beliefs and practices associated with the Christian festivals of Advent, Christmas, Epiphany, Ash Wednesday, Lent, Holy Week (Palm Sunday, Maundy Thursday, Good Friday), Easter, Ascension and Pentecost

✓ know how these festivals relate to the life of Jesus and to events in the life of the early Church

✓ know and understand the observances, customs and symbols connected with these festivals and their meaning for Christians

✓ understand ways in which these festivals impact on the faith and attitudes of the believers

✓ give reasons for and against the continued celebration of these festivals.

Sample answer

1 Write an answer to the following exam question:

Explain how the ceremonies in church on Maundy Thursday might help Roman Catholics to remember what Jesus said and did at the Last Supper.

(6 marks)

2 Read the following sample answer.

> Maundy Thursday is the day before Good Friday. It is the day Catholics remember that Jesus had the Last Supper with his disciples. During this meal Jesus washed the disciples' feet to show how much he loved them. At Mass, the priest washes the feet of twelve people, copying Jesus. After Mass, the priest takes the Blessed Sacrament to the side altar. Here people pray copying Jesus' example in the Garden of Gethsemane before he was arrested.

3 With a partner, discuss the sample answer. Do you think there are other things the student could have included in the answer?

4 What mark would you give this answer out of 6? (Look at the mark scheme in the Introduction on page 7 (AO1) before you attempt this.) What are the reasons for the mark you have given?

AQA Examination-style questions

1 Look at the photographs below and answer the following questions.

(a) Explain how the Advent wreath is used by Roman Catholics. *(3 marks)*

(b) Explain what Christmas celebrates for Christians. *(3 marks)*

 Remember to study the stimulus material carefully and, if appropriate, use information from it in your answer.

(c) 'Advent is a much more important festival than Christmas for Christians.'
Do you agree? Give reasons for your answer, showing that you have thought about more than one point of view. *(6 marks)*

 Remember that you have to present two different points of view, even if you personally believe that one point of view is weak or mistaken. The marks come for the way you present these arguments and the support and evidence you provide for each.

Glossary

A

Adoration: when you show worship.

The Adoration of the Cross: an act of devotion. On Good Friday a wooden cross is laid in front of the congregation and each person comes forward to kiss it.

Advent: the period beginning four Sundays before Christmas and ending on Christmas Eve, in which Christians celebrate the birth of Jesus and look forward to the Second Coming.

Advent wreath: five candles are placed in an evergreen wreath. The outer four (three purple and one pink) are lit on the four Sundays of Advent. The fifth, central, candle (white is lit on Christmas morning.

Aids to worship: items that help Christians to focus when they pray.

Altar: a type of table used for Holy Communion. It is a symbol of the table used by Jesus at the Last Supper.

The Altar of Repose: when the Mass is over on Holy Thursday, the consecrated Bread is taken to the Altar of Repose. This is a side chapel set aside for private prayer to remember Jesus going to the Garden of Gethsemane to pray. People pray privately at this Altar to remind them of the agony of Jesus in the garden and his arrest.

Anglican: a member of the Church of England.

Anointing: being blessed with holy oil.

Apostles: disciples of Jesus who became the leaders of the Early Church. The word means 'sent out'.

Apostles' Creed: a statement setting out the main beliefs of the Christian faith.

Apostolic succession: the belief that the head of Jesus' Church is the Pope and that there has been an unbroken line of succession from St Peter to the current Pope. The Pope (and bishops) inherits the powers Jesus gave to the apostles.

Ascension: the event after the Resurrection, when Jesus returned to God, the Father, in heaven (recorded in Luke 24 and Acts 1); the festival commemorating this event, traditionally on a Thursday 40 days after Easter.

Ash Wednesday: the first day of Lent, a time of penitence. People come to church on this day and have the 'sign of the cross' marked on their foreheads with ashes.

Authority: the power to give orders or to influence people.

B

Baptism: the sacrament through which people become members of the Church. Baptism uses water as a symbol of the washing away of sin. It is a rite of initiation.

Baptistery: a pool used for believers' baptism in a Baptist chapel.

Believers' baptism: initiation into the Church, by immersion in water, of people old enough to understand the ceremony/rite and willing to live a Christian life. Some denominations prefer this to infant baptism.

Bible: sacred book for Christians containing both the Old and New Testaments.

Bishop: a high-ranking clergyman who has the power to confirm and ordain.

Breaking of Bread: alternative name for the Eucharist or Holy Communion.

C

Chapel: a small place of worship, sometimes inside a church; a plain building used instead of a church in some Protestant traditions.

Chrism: holy oil.

Christian: someone who believes in Jesus Christ and follows the religion based on his teachings.

Christmas: the Feast Day commemorating the birth of Jesus (25 December).

Church: the Holy People of God, also called the Body of Christ, among whom Christ is present and active; members of a particular Christian denomination / tradition; a building in which Christians worship.

The Church as the Body of Christ: the belief that the Church is God's people and that it is present wherever people are living a Christian life.

Communion of Saints: all Christian believers, both living and dead.

Confirmation: the sacrament in which the faith of the believer is 'confirmed' or strengthened by the Holy Spirit. Those being confirmed personally confirm their acceptance of the promises made by others at their baptism.

Consecration: the point at which the words of Jesus at the Last Supper are said and the bread and wine become Jesus' Body and Blood.

Consubstantiation: the belief that Christ is present as people receive the bread and wine, but he is not present in the bread and wine.

Creed: a statement of beliefs.

D

Crib: model of a stable, showing the scene of Jesus' birth.

Crucifixion: a form of punishment given by the Romans. The victim is nailed to a cross beam, or tree. Jesus was crucified.

D

Denomination: a distinct group within the Christian faith, with its own organisation and traditions, such as the Roman Catholic, Methodist, Presbyterian and Anglican Churches.

Distribution of ashes: people come to church on Ash Wednesday and have the 'sign of the cross' marked on their foreheads with ashes The ash is a reminder that human beings only have a brief time on earth and a sign that they are really sorry for their sins.

E

Easter: the religious season celebrating the Resurrection of Jesus from the dead. It starts on Easter Sunday and finishes with the feast of Pentecost.

Easter Day: the day when the Resurrection of Jesus is celebrated by Christians.

Easter Sunday: another term for Easter Day.

Easter Vigil: the Roman Catholic main celebration of Easter is on Holy Saturday.

Epiphany: literally 'appearance'. It is a Christian festival held on 6 January in celebration of Jesus as the Messiah and the Son of God. On the feast of the Epiphany, Christians remember the visit of the Magi (the three Wise Men).

Eucharist: literally 'thanksgiving'. Another name for Holy Communion. Thanks are given to God for his creation of the world, for the life, death and Resurrection of Jesus and for the bread and wine which many Christians refer to as Jesus' Body and Blood.

F

Fasting: people fast during Lent as a way of preparing for Easter. Fasting helps Christians to focus on what they really need for survival.

Font: the receptacle in church holding the water used for baptism.

Forgiveness of sins: God's readiness to let people off for the offences they have committed if they are prepared to accept it.

Fundamentalism: belief in the Bible as a factual historical record; miracles are accepted as events that happened exactly as described.

G

Gifts of the Holy Spirit: seven gifts which the Holy Spirit gives to the newly confirmed to help them live full Christian lives. They are wisdom, understanding, right judgement, courage, knowledge, reverence, and wonder and awe.

God the Father: the First Person of the Trinity, the Creator.

God the Holy Spirit: the Third Person of the Trinity, who inspired believers.

God the Son: the Second Person of the Trinity, who took on manhood in Jesus and saved humankind.

Good Friday: the Friday before Easter, when Christians remember the crucifixion and death of Jesus.

Guide: a person who leads you in the right way to safety.

H

Head of the Church: the Pope is the one who tells all Roman Catholics what they ought to believe; he expresses the opinion of the Church.

Holy Communion: another name for the Eucharist in which the sacrificial death and Resurrection of Jesus are celebrated using bread and wine.

Holy Land: the land of Israel / Palestine where Jesus lived, died and rose again.

Holy Saturday: the day between Good Friday and Easter Sunday when Christians remember Jesus among the dead.

Holy Spirit: the third person of the Holy Trinity who descended like a dove on Jesus at his baptism. Christians believe that the Holy Spirit is present and inspires them.

Holy Week: the last week in Lent (the week before Easter Sunday beginning on Palm Sunday), during which believers think about the suffering and death of Jesus.

I

Icon: a religious image of Jesus or one of the saints, used by Orthodox Christians and others. They are seen as being filled with the spirit of the person shown.

Iconostasis: screen covered with icons separating the sanctuary from the nave (the main body) of Orthodox churches.

Immaculate Conception: the belief that the Virgin Mary was conceived in her mother's womb free from sin.

Incarnation: God taking the human form of Jesus.

Infallibility: the principle that the official statements of the Pope are God's will and so cannot be incorrect.

Infant baptism: initiation into the Church of babies and young children,

Initiation: formal entry into a religion.

Inspiration: the guidance from God to write what is in the Bible.

The institution of the Eucharist: at the Last Supper Jesus gave his disciples bread and wine to represent his body and blood. This is the institution of the Eucharist (the first Mass) that is re-enacted at every Mass. Jesus commanded his disciples to 'do this in memory of me' i.e. the institution of the priesthood.

Intercession: when you ask for something, usually on behalf of another person.

Interpretation: an explanation of the meaning (of the Bible).

J

Jesus: first century Jewish teacher and holy man, believed by Christians to be the Son of God.

Judgement: the return of Christ at the end of the world to judge the living and the dead.

L

Last Supper: the final meal that Jesus ate with his disciples, on the evening before his execution. It was based on the Jewish Passover and is the basis of Holy Communion today.

Lay Ministry: a role of service within the Church. All those who are not ordained are expected to serve God and others in their daily lives.

Lectern: a reading desk in a Christian church, chapel or cathedral.

Lent: the 40-day period before Easter, in which Christians are called to pray, fast and give to charity in preparation for Easter. It recalls the 40 days that Jesus spent in the wilderness after his baptism.

Liberal view: the view that the Bible's authors were guided by God, but, being human, they could have made mistakes, meaning that the Bible is not entirely accurate, and need not be taken literally. This approach focuses on the spiritual truth within parables, imaginative stories and accounts of the miracles.

Literalism: a belief that every word of the Bible is literally true, even when this defies common sense and logic (e.g. Mark 16:18).

Liturgical worship: a church service which follows a set text or ritual.

Liturgical year: the annual celebration of major festivals that remind Christians of what God has done.

Liturgy: the set text which religious services follow.

Liturgy of the Eucharist: a form of service centred on the consecrated bread and wine.

Liturgy of the Word: a form of service centred on readings from the Bible.

Lord's Prayer: the prayer taught to the disciples by Jesus; also known as the 'Our Father'.

Lord's Supper: alternative name for the Eucharist or Breaking of Bread.

M

The Magisterium: the teaching authority of the Roman Catholic Church.

Mary: the mother of Jesus. Mary is held in great honour by many Christians as the Mother of God.

Mass: another term for the Eucharist, normally used by Roman Catholics. The rite is divided into two parts, the Liturgy of the Word and the Liturgy of the Eucharist.

The Mass of the Lord's Supper: Christians share in the same meal – just as Jesus' disciples did at the Last Supper. This term is more often used by the Free Churches (Baptists, and Pentecostal Churches, etc.) by doing exactly as Jesus did.

Maundy Thursday: the day before Good Friday, on which Christians remember the Last Supper.

Meditation: being silent and thoughtful in the presence of God.

Meeting House: the place of worship for Quakers.

Memorial: a reminder of past events; for Catholics, making the past a real experience.

Methodist: a non-conformist Protestant Church.

Midnight Mass: the first Mass of Christmas, showing how Jesus brought light into the dark.

Mother of God: an alternative title for Mary, based on the belief that Jesus is God.

N

Nativity: 'birth', the formal title for the Christmas festival.

New Testament: the books of the Bible concerning the life and teachings of Jesus and his followers.

Non-liturgical worship: a service which does not follow a set text or ritual.

O

Old Testament: the books of the Bible, originally written in Hebrew, about the Jews before the time of Jesus. It speaks of God's covenant relationship with his people.

Ordained: appointed as a minister of the Christian Church.

Orthodox: the most popular Christian tradition in some parts of Eastern Europe. Services are heavily traditional and ritualistic.

The Our Father: the name of the Lord's Prayer in Catholic churches. The prayer taught to the disciples by Jesus.

P

Palm Sunday: the first day of Holy Week, when Christians remember Jesus' entry into Jerusalem (recorded in Mark 11:1–11).

Paschal Candle: the candle which is lit on Holy Saturday to symbolise the light of Christ's Resurrection.

The Passion: the term used to describe Jesus' suffering prior to his death.

Pentecost: the day, shortly after the Ascension, when the Apostles felt the presence of the Holy Spirit (recorded in Acts 2:1–4); festival 50 days after Easter, remembering this day.

Peter: the leading Apostle. Peter was the 'Rock' on which Jesus based the Church and was the first pope.

Petition: when you ask for something.

Pilgrimage: a journey by a Christian to a holy site, e.g. Lourdes.

The Pope: the head of the Roman Catholic Church. The successor of Peter who was appointed to lead the Church by Jesus.

Prayer: words of praise, thanks or sorrow, etc. offered to God.

Private worship: a believer giving God praise and worship on his or her own.

Protestant: the Churches that 'protested' against and broke away from the Roman Catholic Church during the Reformation. Services are generally based more closely on the Bible than those of the Roman Catholic and Orthodox Churches.

Psalms: the prayers that are used in Jewish worship which Jesus himself would have used. They are found in the Old Testament.

Public worship: Christians gathering together to praise God.

Pulpit: a raised area in a church from which the sermon is preached.

Q

Quaker: a member of the Society of Friends, a Christian tradition that does not have ministers or a written statement of beliefs. They do not celebrate any of the sacraments.

R

The Resurrection: when Jesus rose from the dead after dying on the Cross. One of the key beliefs of Christianity.

Rite: a ceremony, particularly one following a set structure.

Rites of passage: events which indicate that a person is moving on to a new stage in their life, e.g. baptism, marriage.

Role model: someone who has set a good example on how to act.

Roman Catholic: the tradition within the Christian Church which is led by the Pope.

Rosary: a method of prayer, mainly used by Roman Catholics; the beads used during the praying of the Rosary.

Royal Doors: the doors in the middle of an iconostasis that represent the meeting point between heaven and earth.

S

Sabbath: the first day of the week (Sunday), which Christians set aside for religious observance and rest from work. It was changed from the Jewish Sabbath (Saturday) as Sunday is the day of the Resurrection, the first day of the new creation.

Sacraments: rites and rituals through which the believer receives a special gift of grace, Roman Catholics believe that sacraments are 'outward signs' of 'inward grace'. Different Christian traditions celebrate different sacraments.

Sacrifice: an offering made to God.

Salvation: being saved from, or being freed from, something, such as suffering or the punishment of sin.

Sanctuary: the holy place found in liturgical churches where the altar is placed. Sanctuary lamp: a red lamp which is kept burning to show the Real Presence of Christ in the consecrated hosts in the tabernacle.

Shrine: a holy place of worship or pilgrimage.

Sin: a thought, word or action against the love of God.

Son of God: in mainstream Christianity the title of Son of God is used to describe Jesus as a divine being and a member of the Trinity.

Spontaneous worship: worship which has no set structure, but which allows worshippers to say or do what seems right at the time. Worshippers believe that they are guided in this by the Holy Spirit.

Stations of the Cross: a series of images or pictures in a church of the events of Jesus' trial and execution; a service that remembers the journey of Jesus from Pilate's house to the tomb. It takes place throughout Lent (and at other times), as well as on Good Friday.

Statue: a three-dimensional figure that represents Jesus, Mary or one of the saints.

Steeple: a structure like a tower but one that tapers to a point.

Structured worship: worship which follows a fixed pattern, e.g. Mass has a clear set structure that the priest follows.

Successor to Jesus: Jesus is the leader and the foundation of the Christian faith. Peter took over this role when Jesus had ascended into heaven.

T

Tabernacle: the place in a church where the consecrated Communion bread is usually kept.

Teaching ministry: the function of the Church and its leaders to help believers live by the message of Jesus and to apply it to modern times.

Tower: a tall structure riding above a church to show the importance of the church.

Transubstantiation: the belief that at the Consecration, the bread and wine actually become the Body and Blood of Christ.

Trinity: the belief that there are three Persons in the One God. The Father, Son and Holy Spirit are separate, but are also one being.

U

United service of witness: all the Christian Churches have a united service on Good Friday, often carrying a cross in procession through the main streets. This reminds all people to thank Jesus for the death he suffered for all mankind.

V

Vatican: independent state and centre of Roman Catholicism; papal government.

Virgin Birth: the belief that Mary was a virgin when she gave birth to Jesus and that she had conceived through the power of the Holy Spirit.

W

The washing of the feet: usually 12 parishioners sit at the front of the church and have their feet washed by the priest during the Holy Thursday Mass, a reminder that Jesus washed the feet of his disciples in the Upper Room at the Last Supper. (Jesus gave the disciples a new command (mandatum) to love one another.

Works of mercy: works of mercy are intended to help those people who are in need. Lent can help Christians to share what they have with those people who are worse off than themselves. It is a way of helping Christians to get a right balance in life towards possessions.

Worship: showing respect and value for God.

Index